ROMANCE YOUR GOALS

PLANNING A GENRE FICTION WRITING CAREER

ZOE YORK

CONTENTS

ZoYo Press

London, Ontario, CANADA

www.ZoeYork.com

www.romanceyourbrand.com

DEDICATION

This one is for myself, because positive self-talk has gotten me through the worst of it more than once

ABOUT THIS BOOK

Our publishing business is an extension of who we are and what we want in life. In order to find success at genre fiction writing, authors need to figure out which projects will move them towards their ideal career. In *Romance Your Goals,* New York Times and USA Today bestselling romance author Zoe York lays out a new framework for creating a chain of goals, achievable mile markers that point you in the right direction.

This book includes:

- decision-making tools you can add to your career management toolbox
- further expansion on the Series 2.0 concept, and how progressive career growth can happen without breakout bestseller success
- support for knowing when to take your writing career in a new direction

"A genre fiction writing career is a roller-coaster. The climb is scary. The fall is terrifying. And once I figured out the tricks of it, I fell in love with the ride."

ZOE YORK/AINSLEY BOOTH, USA TODAY & NEW YORK TIMES BESTSELLING AUTHOR

ABOUT THE AUTHOR

Zoe York is a thirteen-time *USA Today* bestselling author of contemporary romance, often with military heroes, and always with scorching heat on the page. Between her two pen names (she also writes erotic romance as Ainsley Booth), she has published more than fifty books since her 2013 debut, *What Once Was Perfect.* Notable career highlights include *Prime Minister* (*USA Today* bestseller twice, in 2016 and 2017), the *SEALs of Summer* anthologies (*New York Times* bestsellers in 2014 and 2015), and the fan favourite Canadian small town series, Pine Harbour and Wardham. She is a mouthy and proud member of Toronto Romance Writers.

facebook.com/zoeyorkwrites
twitter.com/zoeyorkwrites
instagram.com/zoeyorkwrites
youtube.com/zoeyorkwrites

ACKNOWLEDGEMENTS

The whole reason I have written this series of non-fiction books is because people on Twitter seem to like my thoughts on publishing. Thank you to all the enablers.

A special thanks as well to Susan Hayes, who was an early sounding board for the ideas I developed, and my WBF coach, Nikki Haverstock, who kept me focused through multiple existential crises. I appreciate their support!

I also want to thank every author who reached out to me after I gave a presentation at Romance Author Mastermind 2020 with the same title as this book. I hadn't planned on writing a third non-fiction resource, but hearing that my story and the lessons I have learned resonated with my peers gave me the push to expand some of those concepts into what is laid out here. So in turn, I'm very grateful to Skye Warren for hosting RAM, and fostering a community inside which we can have real conversations about what it takes to shoot for the stars.

FOREWORD

If you have read *Romance Your Brand* and *Romance Your Plan,* one of the questions I ask in the first few chapters of this book will be familiar: in five years, what do you want to have written? What do you want to be known for?

I return to it in this book, because I return to it often in real life. As I said in the introduction to *Romance Your Brand,* for me, every day is the first day in a new five-year plan.

That has never been more true than in the two years since I released RYB. My five-year plan in the fall of 2019 did not include a global pandemic, but here we are. So we take stock, revise our vision, and start again.

A genre fiction writing career is a roller-coaster. The climb is scary. The fall is terrifying. And once I figured out the tricks of it, I fell in love with the ride.

But before we dive into goal setting and how this book fits into the Publishing How To series with *Romance Your Brand* and *Romance Your Plan,* I want to establish this as a baseline fact: I'm a peer on this writing and publishing journey.

I'm not an expert on anything other than how to be Zoe

York. I don't do consulting or run a course. These three books are my contribution to the collective knowledge bank, and everything I say should be weighed against the balance of what you know from your own experiences and what you learn from others. *Always be learning* is a great motto! I'm a big fan of treating professional development as an ongoing part of being a commercial genre fiction writer.

In fact, this book is a direct result of some of the professional development I did following the release of *Romance Your Brand*. In November 2019, I attended Romance Author Mastermind in Houston (organized by Skye Warren, whose author newsletter I recommended on the reading list at the back of *RYB*). The year that followed was one of the best, most-focused years I've had as a romance author, even as I navigated the global pandemic (which hit my muse hard, and I'll get into that in a dedicated chapter), in part because I did an author business mastermind with Holly Darling and started to integrate an author mission statement into my process. When RAM 2020 went virtual, and Skye asked me to fill in when a speaker had to back out at the last minute, I knew exactly what I was going to talk about: goals.

That was the first version of *Romance Your Goals*.

And then, *after* I gave that presentation, everyone was talking about HB90 with Sarra Cannon (a quarterly planning week for authors), so I took that course at the end of 2020.

So at this point, in the fall of 2021, as I write this introduction, I can tell you that what you're about to read is a snapshot in time, the perspective of a peer on this journey, captured at the eight and a half year mark into her career.

I can promise that my thoughts about goals will continue to evolve. I will learn new, better, more interesting tools. I will have setbacks.

I have tried to anticipate that in the framework I present in the following chapters. Because I have ridden the rollercoaster a few times now, and I think I have some hot tips for making the ride more enjoyable.

Buckle in.

CHAPTER 1

PUT THE YOU IN ROMANCE YOUR GOALS

I'M GOING to spend a lot of this book talking about myself, and my goals, and I don't want you to mistake any of that for universal advice.

I'm not a goal-setting expert, just as I'm not a brand expert, or a marketing expert.

I'm just a girl with ADHD who communicates entirely in analogies, because I see patterns and really like analysis.

But what really matters as you start this book is that you remember I want you to centre yourself in those analogies. See if they fit. If they feel right, if there are points that resonate, highlight them and make them your own.

If there is anything that doesn't feel right, that's important, too. It might remind you of other times that items have snuck onto your to-do list that aren't *yours.* I want to explicitly encourage you to de-prioritize anything doesn't excite you, anything that doesn't advance you closer to what you really want out of this career.

Okay, back to me.

As I worked on a presentation for my colleagues at Romance Author Mastermind, I realized that the thing that had made my career so stable—not sexy, not breakout, but steady income every single month—was my unwavering commitment to the goal of having steady income every single month.

And you might think, but Zoe, I want that, too. And I don't have it.

I hear you. But I'll also tell you that there are other goals I have set for myself over the years that I have *wanted*, and not achieved.

There is a world of difference between **wanting something**, and feeling **a bone-deep unwavering commitment to the goal of having something.**

In some ways, what I'm going to talk about in this book is not strictly speaking, new. It builds on principles that I first introduced in *Romance Your Brand* and repeated again, in *Romance Your Plan*.

Now we're going to put those together in a five-step plan:

- Step one, figure out where you want to go
- Step two, assess whether or not you have already taken some steps in that direction
- Step three, build a plan to get there
- Step four, gather the tools and the team that will help you get there
- Step five, do the work to get there

The job of being a Genre fiction writer is writing. Over and over again, producing books for the market. It's staring at that blank page, having the thought, "I don't know how to write a book, how did I ever do this before?" and doing it anyway. It's quite the marvellous talent we have, and yet we're often riddled with self-doubt.

That doubt is your biggest hurdle some days.

Doubt will whisper lies to you about your goals. It will muddy your analysis. It will sabotage your efforts to build a plan. It will stop you from reaching out to a partner for success. And it will stop you from doing the work to get where you want to go.

This book may be a lot to take in all at once. If at any point you feel overwhelmed, or like I'm pushing you too fast, feel free to put it down and come back later. Monuments are not built in a day, or a week, or even a year. This book will be here whenever you're ready to take the next step, or when you want to rebuild, review, or start over.

And finally, I want to say something about privilege.

There's a line in Celeste Ng's *Little Fires Everywhere* that I've seen quoted all over the place. (I haven't read the book, or seen the show, but I often see the quote shared without attribution, so I looked it up and now the attribution is seared on my brain.) "You didn't make good choices. You *had* good choices."

Privilege is often labelled as luck. We cannot have a real conversation about goals without also unpacking the way privilege makes it easier to build a path toward those goals. Some of us are starting with more tools available to us, and some of us operate more fluently in the spaces where white stories and stories of privilege are rewarded.

But even having privilege of having good choices doesn't mean you can make them. Sometimes, we want something and it still zooms right on past while we think really hard about how much we wanted it.

(If you are someone who right now feels like you chronically watch good choices zoom by, maybe skip right ahead to the Baby Steps chapter, then come back.)

And for those authors who are starting in a marginalized place, I want to underline the importance of supportive peers. Peers who look like you, and colleagues who are starting from a similar place. I often see discussion around mentorship, but I don't think we talk nearly enough about the importance of finding a cohort. This is true in general—and I dig into that in a later chapter—but it's extra true for marginalized writers. You will be told over and over again that your work is niche, that there isn't a broad audience for it. One way to combat those external messages is to surround yourself with people who are creating similar work, who *are* that audience. They will show you that the niche is bigger than the gatekeepers think.

TEN STEPS TO A PRIVATE ISLAND

I'm the author of 50-something romances and two non-fiction books. I started publishing in June 2013, and my first book was a Christmas romance. Take that as your first reminder that I'm just a peer on this journey of figuring everything out.

But over the last eight years, I've set a number of goals, and achieved every single one that I really truly committed myself to. (I've half-assed a couple of goals, and the results were less than stellar.)

In brainstorming how to approach the original presentation version of this material, I joked to a friend that this talk could be called, **Ten Steps to Getting Out Of Your Own Way**. Maybe, **Ten Steps to Career Longevity**, or, if we're being lofty, **Ten Steps to A Private Island.**

(The last title will make sense when we dig into my own goals in chapter nine)

But the truth is, I'm not sure it's **ten steps** to any of those goals. *I do know they are possible.* But for each of us, that kind of ultimate freedom will be a different number of steps away. Whatever your private island is, your early retirement, your full end-cap of books ... that goal is possible, but the plan to get there will be uniquely yours and only you can figure out how many intermediate goals or progress markers exist between here and there.

This is why I call my non-fiction books, *Romance* ***Your***

Brand and *Romance* ***Your*** *Plan*. And it's why I call this book, *Romance* ***Your*** *Goals.*

And because everyone likes a good numbered list, I have refined the ten steps into five broader ones. Inside those five steps, you can add as many sub-steps as you need.

There is no time limit on figuring out a successful path to your goals.

The only person you are in competition with in this industry and in your career is you. Past you, future you. Can you get ahead? Can you keep up? Can you finish this book energized and fired up to make the next year your best year yet?

What I can encourage you to do is that: analyze your own successes, AND your failures. Spend more time observing yourself than others, but every so often, lift your head and look around. Make note of what you like when you see it. Start to build a "Potentially Could Do That To Level Up" list.

But before you can dive into a to-do list, it's worth stepping back and really analyzing where you come from and what you value, so you know that you're picking action items that align with your true vision and secret, inner goals.

MY EARLY CHILDHOOD was framed by a kind of poverty that is hard to properly capture. I spent the first few years of my life living off-grid in rough structures my parents built themselves. One winter, my grandparents—immigrant farmers—paid for an apartment above a garage so me and my infant sister wouldn't have to spend the winter in an uninsulated stone cottage.

My parents split up when I was eight. My life got better after that, safer, and my mom's business grew year over year. But I was a teenager before we owned a television. And when the fuel tank ran out in March, we made do with the woodstove.

To me, "making it" is about stability. That upper middle-class ease of regular holidays and not having to juggle unexpected bills across credit cards.

In 2015, I bought a new-to-me car, a 2011 Ford Escape, and I paid cash for it without a second thought. I have taken my family on vacations around the world—flying coach, of course, because I cannot imagine anything else. To me, that *is* making it.

And it's not just childhood trauma that informs my worldview and career goals. Because of how attractive I find stability, my first career was in education. I worked at a university for almost a decade, in a career with a salary and benefits. And then I was promoted into a newly created position, to lead a new project that never came to fruition.

It was a move I thought would increase my stability. Instead, it was a right-hand turn into a dead end, and I found myself writing in the evenings and on weekends to find some passion where my career was no long satisfying me.

A year and a half later, the position was eliminated, and I was laid off.

That was May 1, 2014. The start of a new fiscal year for the university. And, it turned out, the start of a new life for me, because the day before, April 30, 2014, I had found out that a romance collection, *SEALs of Summer*—containing a novella I wrote—hit the *New York Times* bestseller list at #6. It also hit the *USA Today* bestseller list at #22—and it would stay on the *USAT* list for four weeks.

That was my first time goalling for a list, and we had done it in style.

I had four books out, and wasn't earning full-time money yet from my writing. Not consistently.

I had a severance package that would give me a number of

months to look for a new job, but deep down, I knew I didn't need a new job. I had a new career already—but it's one that often comes with a roller coaster of financial ups and downs.

Little Miss Stability had a new goal: ten months to full-time income, every single month.

Romance Your Goals

- [ ] Step one:
  figure out where you want to go

- [ ] Step two:
  assess whether or not you have already taken some steps in that direction

- [ ] Step three:
  build a plan to get there

- [ ] Step four:
  gather the tools and the team that will help you get there

- [ ] Step five:
  do the work to get there

CHAPTER 2

BUT WHAT DO YOU REALLY WANT?

BEING LAID off is a traumatic event I don't wish on anyone, but I can't deny that it was a significant, reframing moment in my career. In an instant, what I wanted and my options for getting there changed radically.

Up to that point, what I wrote had largely been driven by what I wanted to write, and the novelty of challenges proposed by my writing acquaintances.

But when faced with the choice of looking for another job, or turning this newfound opportunity into a real, supporting-my-family type of career, I chose door number two.

Which meant I also needed to shift up what I was writing, because while I had experienced some taste of success, I knew that my baseline wasn't enough to replace my full-time income.

Years after this moment, I would take Becca Syme's Write Better Faster class and figure out that I have some natural strengths in the areas of reflection and analysis.

If you don't have these strengths, and want to borrow them from me, here is a replay of the conversation I had in my head that day (to the best of my recollection).

I could write full time.
Oh crap, writing full time means writing needs to be my full time income.
Is that doable?
I did have one very good month after BookBub featured my first book for free.
But then sales slid the month after.
Sales do that, Zoe. They go up and down. That's the business model you're about to embrace with both arms.
Right. So I need more series. So when one goes down, the other can be going up.
How many series do I need? Probably six, right? So I can be promoting one every other month?
I'm five series short. Probably can't create those overnight. What do I already have? This one Navy SEAL novella in that boxed set.
That's okay. That's the start of your second series.
But it's totally different from the small town series.
So we need a third series. One that's a bridge between them. Small town military romance.
A new series. Right.
Three series is a good start. If we alternate promoting a free book and a new release, that's all we need to have six peaks a year.
Can we make a full-time living off six marketing events a year?
Better get writing.

There's a lot of panic and hyperventilating that I'm leaving out, but all of that really did roll through my head that first week of being a full-time writer. Let's pull out the key questions:

- How many series or projects do I need so I can be promoting [at my preferred frequency]?
- What do I already have?
- If I alternate promotions with new releases, how many marketing events do I have in a year?
- Can I meet my goals with this plan?

I actually already knew, instinctively, what my goals were—I was on the path to writing in series already. At this point in May 2014 I had four books (three novels and a novella) in my Wardham small town series, and a novella in the *SEALs of Summer* boxed set.

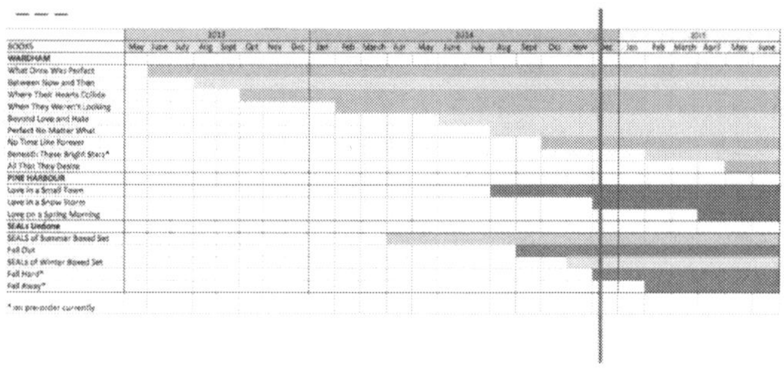

If this chart is too small to read, you can find it on my website:

www.romanceyourbrand.com/romance-your-goals/

and a larger copy is included in the Appendix at the back of this book

The screenshot above is from a presentation I gave in December 2014, talking about the plan I had come up with in that intense first week of May, and by the time of the presentation had successfully implemented. The vertical line on the graph represents where I was at the time of the presentation:

my first series had three more titles added to it, the first SEAL book had been re-released as a new first in series, and I'd written another SEAL book and released that in a new boxed set (SEALs of Winter, which repeated our hit to the USA Today bestseller list).

But the most important part of this chart is the series in the middle. In August of 2014, I launched my Pine Harbour series, which is that mash-up of the two other series in my catalogue.

But it wasn't just pulling what I thought readers like best from those two existing elements of my catalogue. It was also about trying to orient the first in series as best I could to the centre of a sub-genre, to position it well so that down the road, when I made it a free first in series, it would be a strong funnel entry point.

That book is called *Love in a Small Town*, and eight years later, I'm still writing in Pine Harbour. At the time of publication, I'm working on the twelfth book in this town, in a second series, and I have a third series planned after this one.

Pine Harbour was my first Series 2.0, a concept I'll come back to later in this book. But right now, I want to focus on that vertical line on that graph. December 2014 was an important milestone, and not just because the plan that I had put into place was finally working. But—and I didn't know this at the time that I made the chart on the previous page—it would actually turn out to be the start of a very long stretch of success for me.

It was both the end of a plan, and first step in a new stage of my career.

And in hindsight, I can track that back to goals I had instinctively set for myself.

LAST SUMMER I gave a presentation to a wonderful group of writers, and someone I have known in online circles since before I released my first book said to me (and I'm only paraphrasing slightly), "It was like you just came out of nowhere, and then you were everywhere."

This is the nicest compliment anyone has ever given me, it truly made my day, and was not at all what my first six months of publishing felt like on the inside. Also, objectively speaking, I don't think my earliest numbers bear that assessment up, either, but it doesn't matter. That was her perspective, and what it does accurately reflect is my enthusiasm and hustle at the time.

And by December 2014, it was probably true. The first eleven months of my career (June 2013 to April 2014) were totally different from the next seven months.

I'm quite proud of that! I also don't always feel capable of either enthusiasm or hustle these days, so it's sort of like looking back on youthful fitness and thinking, oh, you didn't appreciate your flexibility enough when you had it.

I didn't appreciate my assent from debut author to unexpected bestseller to full-time author nearly enough, because the whole time I was busy comparing myself to others—and feeling like I was coming up short in every corner. Even today, knowing that what I have accomplished in my career so far is objectively quite decent, my brain sneakily adds in, *but it's not as much as other people. So many people don't know your name at all. So many people...*

You get the picture. That whole time I was figuring out my clear objective and building a plan that would come to fruition right on schedule, setting myself up for long-term success...I was also being mean to myself.

The thing is, in being mean to myself, I was also contributing to some of the toxic narratives we perpetuate in publishing: that it's all or nothing, that the only success which matters is outlier success, and attempts that fall short of an arbitrary mark are failures to be thrown out.

There are so many different ways a book can be successful. Sometimes I see gatekeepers in traditional publishing (agents and editors) perpetuating myths that block people from viable careers, particularly the idea that books are either hits or not.

Books can be successful:

- out of the gate
- years after release
- in digital only
- primarily in print
- as bestsellers
- as niche evergreen sellers
- as quiet backlist books
- as a stepping stone to different success down the road
- as learning opportunities
- as catharsis

And in this early retrospective review, we can see a lot of that. My first book wasn't a success. But by December 2014, it was an important part of my plan to have a rotating group of free catalogue entry points.

(For that matter, *Love in a Small Town* wasn't overly successful when I launched it in August of 2014, only selling 400 copies in release month—still an improvement over What Once Was Perfect did—but by early 2015, it would drive thousands of sales across my catalogue.)

So wherever you are at right now, as you dig into this work of refining your goals, I want to encourage you to be kind to yourself. Right now, there is someone out there watching you with awe. They are impressed with what you have done, and if you are busy beating yourself up for not keeping up with someone else's plan, you won't realize that person is right.

What you have already accomplished is amazing. And it's a part of your journey to where you want to go next.

The next couple of chapters are going to focus on step one of this plan: figuring out where you want to go.

Before we dive into them, I want to share a caveat. If you already have a plan, some of what we explore next may reveal cracks. It's important to know when to stick to a plan, and when to leap in a new direction. My friend Susan Hayes said this perfectly when I was brainstorming this book with her, so I asked her if I could quote her verbatim: "One of the things writers need to hear is that everything is flexible. Today's plan may not be tomorrow's. And being too attached to a plan is counter productive."

It's so true. She went on to describe what I talk about in my workshops as "how to build the foundation" of a good writing career, which I love. Thank you, yes, I want that for everyone. But she also pointed out the importance of knowing "when to change the blueprints."

I do love a clear analogy!

So let me expand on that a little. Never be afraid of identifying cracks in that foundation. Cracks can be repaired, and foundations can be re-poured.

Okay, sometimes they have created such structural instability that what is truly required is a new foundation. Curse you, very good analogy. Curse you and your keen insight.

So now I'm going to ask you a question I've asked you before (if you've read my other books, or attended a workshop, or if you read the foreword of this book):

Five years from now, what do you want to have written?

CHAPTER 3

THE FIVE YEAR QUESTION

ON MAY 1, 2014, I didn't explicitly ask myself this question, but in my retrospective analysis, I can see that I was clearheaded about where I wanted to go. That day, looking at what I had written, I knew that the next step I wanted to take was to start a new series, a small town military romance series that I would write in for years to come.

In other words, I knew that five years down the road, I wanted to be known as an author of small town military romance.

"Five years from now, what do you want to have written? What do you want to be known for?" I have now asked this question in countless workshops, to hundreds if not thousands of other writers.

Sometimes it resonates. Sometimes it doesn't.

One question I get a lot is, what if I can't answer this question?

And the variations to that are:

What if I don't know where I want to be five years from now?

What if I don't know what I want to have written five years from now?

I would ask you back: why don't you know?

Why did you pick up this book?

Why are you seeking answers?

If you can't work through the exercise of imagining where you want to be, it might be that five years is not the right number for you. You can do the same exercise for three years.

You can do a form of this exercise at one year, but I have learned over the last couple of years that one year is only enough time to *get started* down a path. It is a rare writer who can write enough genre fiction products to achieve life-changing goals within a year. That's not the business that we're in.

And that right there might be one of the problems! Some of the barriers that stand between us and answering this question are fantasies about what we wish this business was.

We might wish that it will be a single book that changes our life, that we become known as The Author of One Title. And on the strength of that project, we are thrust into great outlier success.

That is generally speaking, a fantasy. Not what being a commercial genre fiction writer is.

For most of us, commercial genre fiction is a step-by-step journey through endless publication. Not necessarily frequent publication, although sometimes it is. It could be as infrequent as one book a year or even less, one book every other year. But even those who write a book every other year, the business plan underlying the dream is that you will keep doing that over and over and over again until you retire.

If you can't look at those projects laying in front of you and map out where they're going to go, if you can't pick a touch-stone moment down the road and point in that direction, then you might need an ally on this journey to do that for you. An agent, a manager, a writing partner... someone who can bring that kind of guidance to your plan.

But after reading what I've just said, perhaps there's something inside of you that has been shaken loose. Perhaps there's something that can work its way around those barriers and wave a little hand and say hi, I'm your secret goal. I'm the goal that you didn't want to look right in the eye because I seem too lofty. Or, I'm the goal that you ignored because I seemed too modest. Either way, if something has pricked your conscience, pick that goal—just for now—just for the purposes of this exercise. And after we work through the whole exercise, after you've read the whole book, maybe cycle back to this and do this exercise again.

As I have said in the past, every single day can be the first day of a new five year plan.

Nothing is locked in stone.

Running through this exercise is something that I want you to do on a semi-regular basis. Anytime you need to touch base with yourself, you can ask yourself this step one set of questions:

Five years from now, what do I want to have written? What do I want to be known for?

And to properly answer that, we might need to do some of the dreaded comparison to others. Because writing goals are not universal. In fact, each of us has a unique goal profile.

CHAPTER 4

KNOW YOUR GOAL PROFILE

IN *ROMANCE YOUR BRAND,* I outlined an exercise I called "Tap Into Your Enthusiasm", which connects how we see ourselves as writers to what we love to write, and formalizing that as a mission/vision statement to write towards.

TAP INTO YOUR ENTHUSIASM EXERCISE

1. Mission: Who you are, what you write, and maybe who you write it for. You and your genre.
2. Vision: What you love. Your favourite tropes, sub-genres, archetypes, and story structures.
3. Action Plan: Put *that* on the page. Nothing else. Harness your enthusiasm and write exactly what you want to write, in the form that is most compatible with commercial fiction.

Now I want to refine this exercise and make it as specific to you as we possibly can, by adding some context around this in regards to what you want to do with those stories after you put them on the page.

This chapter used to be much longer, and now I've narrowed it down, because the last thing I want to do here is ask you to fit yourself into one of seven Author Types as I define them. Rather, I want to tell you how *I* see authors around me, and why I think it's helpful to differentiate how and when they have different goals.

The first difference that usually is noticed these days in romance writing circles is "trad vs indie". Do you want to find an agent and sell a book to a publisher (trad) or do you want to learn how to self-publish your book directly to the various ebook retailers (indie)?

But sometimes a trad author who writes long cowboy series has more in common with an indie author who does the same, both releasing multiple novels a year, compared to a trad or indie author who focuses their energy (and that of a significant team) on one or two major launches.

In 2022, trad vs indie is the wrong distinction for the most part. There are some outlier success paths that can only be achieved with a major print distribution plan (but I see indie authors scoring that after solo successes) and there are some amateur publishing choices that New York won't touch (but I see trad authors doing them slyly on the side under secret pen names).

The better comparison to make, and only for the sake of clarity around your own goals, is about what you want that path to look like. Not the label, but the specifics.

- how many projects do you want to work on in a year
- what kind of support team do you need
- what kind of revision on your books feels right
- what kind of acquisition process feels right

So much of this is *what feels right*, and there are two ways to figure that out: observing *all* the options, and doing the ones that intrigue you.

What are those options? I call them **goal profiles**. What is most important to underline is that they are not fixed; writers can start out with one set of goals, or because of no clear goals, spend time in one kind of career space, then morph into another. There is overlap and maturation.

Sometimes there is a fundamental market shift that tips everything sideways and propels someone into a new space, and new options present themselves. (See, everyone who catapulted from fan fiction writing into big trad publishing contracts; see also, anyone who used to have big trad sales numbers and has now found a different kind of happiness in midlist indie publishing.)

GOALS PROFILES AS ZOE SEES THEM

Outlier
Singular products, launched into the stratosphere; fandom drives itself

Bestseller
Progressive, cumulative growth with sustained success at the top of the rollercoaster ride

Award-winning Author
Might overlap with Bestseller or Artist; focused on peer or industry acknowledgement of craft excellence

Artist
My way or the highway, because my way is precious

Midlist

Consistency trumps celebrity, let's do this thing

Hobbyist

Another career dominates, but I take this seriously

Amateur

Editing? I don't need no stinking editing

I don't want to define these goal profiles in too much detail. It will be more meaningful if you define them for yourself, if you start to distinguish *your* goal profile from what you see in your peers and colleagues, or here in my list, and what you think of those labels.

I tested this theory, by workshopping this list in a few circles. And each time, as I gave examples of what I meant by an outlier or a hobbyist, we hit a stumbling block because some of those people—all people I respect—did not agree with my definition of those labels.

They mean something different to each person.

And that makes sense. We are each standing at a specific point in our journey, with all the knowledge from our career to date. We also carry all of our hopes and dreams for what will come.

So for somebody who fits the goal profile of an outlier, if my definition of what that is does not match with their self-identity, that is going to be a friction point.

There's also a chance that my list is incomplete. (A chance? A certainty.)

I could list seven or ten or fifteen different goal profiles here and not perfectly capture you. You might fall in between two, or feel that you straddle two, and that's okay. The most useful part of this exercise is just understanding that we're not all the same. That we all want different things. And the sooner we let go of what other people want, the sooner we can embrace what it is that we do want.

Careers run a gamut, and there are plans to get to the peak of whatever terrifying mountain or gentle rolling hill you feel like climbing.

I WANT TO SPEAK, though, privately, to the people who see themselves at the far end of this spectrum. If you don't think that you have the goal profile of an outlier, that you don't want to wait for The Deal that will change everything, then skip this part.

There is this idea out there in marketing that the time of the mega blockbuster is over, and that the path to success is in finding your niche. Finding a thousand fans is the new hot advice—super fans that will support you that will subscribe to your Patreon or fund your Kickstarter. And that is one approach to marketing that works for some people. That works for some goal profiles, but not for others because there are still people who either want to have that mega blockbuster, and in publishing, we still see them. They are the books that are sold at auction. They're the books that have such a substantial advance that they have a matching marketing budget. And in the indie sphere, these are the books that people bet the house on—and while that makes me feel a little faint, I don't want you to ever think you shouldn't shoot for the moon if that is what makes you absolutely happy.

ON THE OTHER end of the spectrum, there are people who are still figuring out what it is that they want to do. So they are more like dabblers, and the thought of committing to anything, but especially committing to a group of fans when who knows where they will want to be in five years, is Not Good. I'm not entirely sure why a dabbler might have picked up this book, but if that is you, and you're just writing to have a good time, and maybe you're curious...that's great. Thank you for reading this far. Celebrate your own unique goal profile, friend. You want what you want, and maybe your plan is a single step: have fun.

WHEREVER YOU DECIDE you fall in terms of what you really want, make sure that your circle of influence, your network of peers, and your mentors or who you go to for advice all understand and celebrate your goals, and at least some of those people share them.

Being alone in having a goal is hard. Even with strong boundaries, it can be impossible to protect yourself from the conflicting advice out there that is driven by and serves not-your-goals. Those tactics and advice aren't *wrong* per se, but they aren't right for you. And not just because you don't like them, or they feel wrong, but because they do not align with your long term vision for your career.

So in addition to the Tap Into Your Enthusiasm exercise, we can now do a Protect Your Enthusiasm exercise, too.

PROTECT YOUR ENTHUSIASM EXERCISE

1. Position: Where you stand in publishing, and where you want to land. This is your road map.
2. Priorities: The principles of publishing that resonate, the lifestyle you want, the writing craft and publishing choices that fill you with excitement.

3. Strategic Plan: Harness your enthusiasm and take steps to make those goals a reality. Nothing else. Make progressive steps toward where you want to land, using this framework as a benchmark.

The first exercise, that I wrote about in *Romance Your Brand,* is really about what you write. What goes on the page. This second part is more about the business and career choices we make. The goal here is to figure out where we want to go, and consciously letting go of what other people think we should do.

People who have opinions about what I should write include: my mother-in-law, my sister, my best friend, my colleagues, my readers, random people on Twitter.

People whose opinions about what I should write really matter: just me*.

* Now, if you're pursuing an agent right now, or you have an agent and you're working on projects to pitch to editors, you might be frowning at this.

Or maybe you're self-published and in it for the money. Literally, you are happy to write whatever is trending right now.

(These two things are the same, by the way)

It still comes down to you. You will still need enthusiasm for that priority choice. And if you don't have it, or if you have lost it, come back to this first step and figure out what has changed.

You are not going to please every other writer out there with your choices. You don't need a stamp of approval from editors or agents who don't share your vision. Stop trying to live up to someone else's goals. Stop constraining yourself, and start publishing with enthusiasm only. Write the books you want, make the deals you want, and centre yourself in the decision making process.

CHAPTER 5

LEARN TO CHECK IN WITH YOURSELF

I'VE SPENT a lot of time so far talking about the Five Year Question. That's **long term goal work** (and so is the Tapping Into Your Enthusiasm exercise). That is what I intuitively did the day I was laid off. In more recent years, I've taken a couple of excellent professional development classes focused on **short term goal work**, and the stand out there is Sarra Cannon's HB90 bootcamp, which I highly recommend.

But there's another set of goal exercises that falls in between, and I call these **mid-range goal work**.

These have no fixed schedule. You can tap into them whenever you feel yourself drifting off course. For me, I find I need to do them once or twice a year, and if I'm struggling to stay focused on my work or cannot seem to readily pull together quarterly goals, then that's a sure sign that I need to do some mid-range goal work.

I break these into four categories: semi-annual review, priorities review, maintenance check-in, and maximization planning.

Here is an overview of where they sit in between the other two categories of goal work.

LONG TERM GOAL WORK

- Where are you heading, what do you want to be known for
- Mission and vision exercises

SHORT TERM GOAL WORK

- Quarterly planning

MID-RANGE GOAL WORK

- semi-annual review
- priorities review
- maintenance check-in
- maximization planning

The reason I put this at the end, and not in between the other two types of work, is because it's what I came to last in my journey to better understand myself and my business goals. Mid-range goal work is all about refinement and analysis, and that requires a good amount of personal data. Experience, in other words. Trial and error, work that has gone well and work that hasn't, and all of your feelings around those different experiences.

So when it comes to figuring out where you want to go, I suggest you do the work in three stages.

Always start with the longest range vision you can muster (one year, three year, five year, lifetime goals, whatever). Then figure out what you can do in the next little while that will point you in that direction (three months is a business quarter, hence "quarterly planning" being popular). And as you get into a flow of work that starts to feel like you're getting some traction, then pause every so often to check in.

SEMI-ANNUAL REVIEW

This is exactly what it sounds like. If you tend to orient yourself to a calendar year for big goal planning, don't be surprised if mid-year you need a check-in to confirm that those goals still resonate, or discover they need some tweaking.

PRIORITIES REVIEW

This kind of mid-range goal work is more about the underpinnings of our plans. Do we still value what drove us to pick our big goals? Has anything happened in our personal lives or the larger world that might destabilize goals built on previously held priorities?

MAINTENANCE CHECK-IN

This is similar to a semi-annual review, but more focused on the habits and routines that support our writing. Are we happy with the tools we use? How about the team we have collected to support us? This kind of mid-range goal work can also be filed under *burnout prevention.*

MAXIMIZATION PLANNING

This is almost goal pre-work. This is what I do when I hear about something new (most recently, it was about translations as an investment-to-income pillar), and I want to explore it as an option before I cement it into the overarching plan, mapped to my long-term goals.

. . .

A USEFUL TOOL for any self-check in is an Eisenhower Decision Matrix, or an Eisenhower Box. A four square grid, this compares two priority values and rates work on a scale of 1 to 4, where 1 meets both of the priority factors, and 4 meets neither of them. This tool has been widely explored in many self-help books and courses, with different labels on the two axis sides. The original labels come from a quote from Dwight D. Eisenhower: "I have two kinds of problems, the urgent and the important. The urgent are not important, and the important are never urgent."

But some tasks are both urgent and important, and sorting your to-do list or dream idea list can reveal which are (and ergo, which should have top priority).

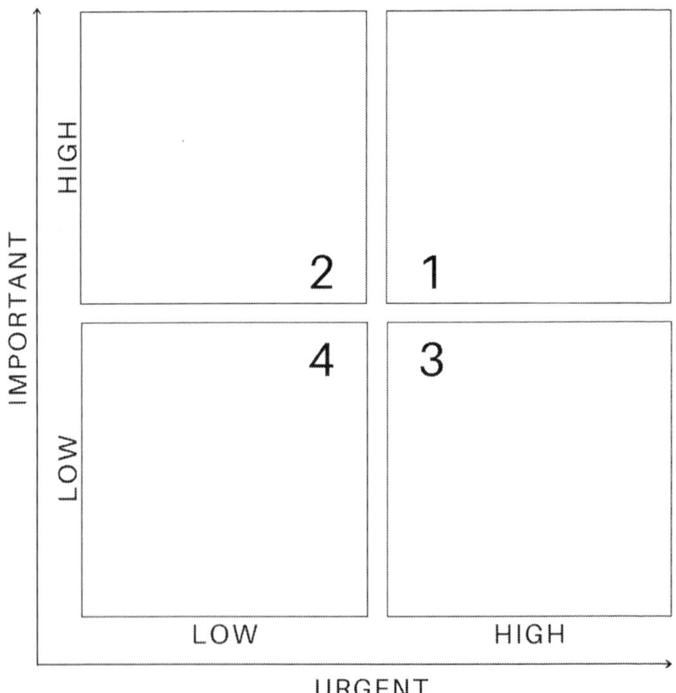

You can swap in any axis labels that move you. Another pair I've seen a lot is Impact and Effort, and one I'm playing with myself lately is Aspirations and Strategic.

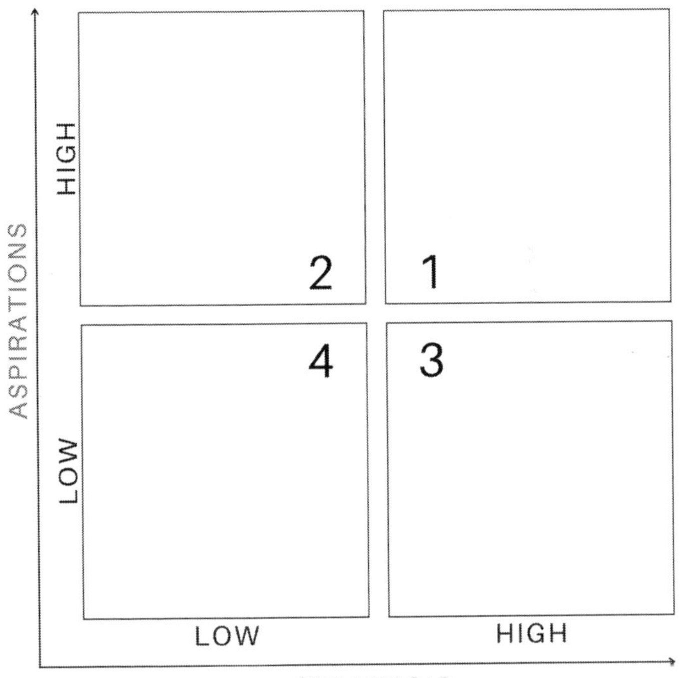

I go back and forth on which axis to put Strategic vs Aspirations. And I played around with Inspiration instead of Aspirations. It really depends where you decide your top priority is: your art or your business? There is no wrong answer here.

(If you want an in-depth walk through on how to use an Eisenhower Matrix, I recommend Sarra Cannon's HB90 class and Roni Loren's Fighting for Focus: Productivity for Writers class, both of which use this tool in different ways)

Doing this kind of periodic check-in will have multiple

benefits for you. Not only will it refine and improve your goals, but it will also teach you some transferrable skills. Because once you can look at your goal work more objectively, then you will probably be able to also look at your catalogue of creative work with a similar objectivity. And that's the first part of step two: assessing if you have already taken steps in the direction of these goals.

CHAPTER 6

YOU'VE DONE MORE THAN YOU THINK

STEP two and step three of this book are two parts of a whole: we want to take the time to map out the career that we want and research the steps it takes to get there, but we should also plot out what we have already done before we re-invent the wheel.

I encourage you to do this step because for me, what has made the difference between a writing dream and a writing career—what has given me long term income stability—is embracing both quiet and loud successes.

NASCENT FANDOM

One of the hardest lessons I have had to learn as an author is that I don't always recognize nascent fandom when it is happening. In hindsight, it is easier to see.

But at the time, the origins of fandom—the little tiny blips of metrics—are not impressive. Part of this is about the phenomenon of us comparing ourselves as a work in progress to someone else's mature career. We compare ourselves at twelve, eighteen, or twenty-four months into our writing career to somebody who is twelve, eighteen, or twenty-four years into their writing career.

When I was first published, it was Jill Shalvis or Robin Carr that I aspired to be. It was their releases that I compared mine to.

Of course, mine were not impressive in comparison.

So of course, I had doubt about whether or not the books that I was writing resonated at all with that target audience.

Even when I had some early reviews from people I did not know that compared me to those authors, I did not believe it, because that was just one review on one book and another single review on a different book.

Even when I started to collect readers in my reader group on Facebook, I did not believe that my books were hitting the market. The way that they "should" … because it was only forty readers that I collected. It was only a hundred people that I had on my mailing list after months of trying.

One of the hardest things to learn is that at the beginning, it takes a monumental effort to move the needle even a tiny little bit down the road. Once you go through that monumental effort over and over and over again, suddenly—at some point that is not predictable in the slightest—it becomes easier to move that needle. But up until that point, it is a lot of effort for very small reward.

So we need to look at that very small reward in as analytical a way as possible. And find in that very small reward some real data, some measurable metrics that will show us that we are on the right track that we are in fact writing books that do connect with readers.

ANOTHER HARD LESSON for me to learn is that not every idea I want to write is monetizable.

The value of my output is variable.

Debut books are wildly uneven in quality. Some are amazing; some are good; others have excellent bones, and captivating premises, but the writing falls short of the mark. Some are technically proficient, but lack a certain hooky spark.

And then there may be a point in your writing career where you run out of juice, or your commercial and artistic instincts fall out of sync.

My lowest income year (after 2013) was 2018, when I published pretty much nothing but women-loving-women shorts in anthologies and a SEALs at Summer Camp story; Pine Harbour residual income and one PH release definitely saved my butt.

Everything before the semi-colon in that paragraph was not monetizable (by me). It doesn't mean there's anything fundamentally unsellable about that content[1], or my writing, but it wasn't a business-aligned decision.

But how do I know that?

I can analyze that now, in a good year, with years of space and a nerdy addiction to data. And, more importantly, *other* data, ie, books that do sell.

Until you hit upon a success, how are you supposed to know what success feels like, and move towards it?

I can't promise that it will feel the same for you as it does for me, but for what it's worth, this is my understanding at this point in my career: while I can't guess which of my next books will be hits and which will be misses, there is a better chance that the ones that fill me with a sizzling kind of fear are going to hit the mark rather than the ones that feel safe.

The tricky part of that is that when you first start publishing, every book feels that way. It's an absolute rush to write a book, a whole book, something that felt impossible until you did it. And then to get that book polished and into a final form?

It's art.

It's love.

It's imperfect perfection, and you hold it so dear that there's no way to objectively stand back from it and say, "that was safe."

Instead, we oscillate between extremes. Before it releases, we think it's so very good. And then, once it's out (or maybe just before), we are convinced it's pretty bad. There may be a rush after release, some very nice reviews. It's good again.

(Some of you don't experience the whims of the market quite so fiercely, but I'll get to you, hang in there with me.)

And then the first sharp review.

Most recently for me, it wasn't even a review. It was an unexplained three-star rating, after someone reached out to me asking for an extra-early copy of a book to hit a review deadline pre-release.

No review was forthcoming. Just the first rating on the book, three unexplained stars. The book wasn't worthy of a review, I guess.

The book inexplicably slid to being bad again in my mind.

And we—I—spend a lot of time in this "is my book good or bad" space, enough time that it starts to morph into "am *I* good or bad?" And not just as a writer, but also maybe as a person. (My therapist says the difference between regret and shame is regret is feeling like I've made a mistake, and shame is feeling like I am a mistake. Whew, I felt that one hard.)

But if we refuse these words, *good* and *bad,* because those are external to us and our work...and if we instead say, *safe* and *exciting,* does the relationship to the question shift?

If I miss the mark on exciting, and merely make a book that is safe, there may be some regret there, but no shame.

For one thing, there is actually a market for safe books! They don't really set the world on fire, but they are nice to read.

For another thing, it is much easier to pivot from safe to

exciting than it is from bad to good. And at some point, you will want to pivot.

But also, you might—when you turn the page and see what I ask you to do next—be tempted to go back and change some of your earlier books. I have done this. Let me spare you the energy and encourage you to mostly not bother.

Books are what they are. The ways we can modify them don't actually take them from X to Y (okay to spectacular, etc.).

We often set an impossibly high standard for ourselves, both for the work and separately for the results we want from that work, when it's all just weird alchemy with the market and readers. Tons of non-spectacular books do well, and many spectacular books crash and burn. I read a book the other day that I thought was the best thing since sliced bread, and two reader acquaintances DNFed[2] it. What if it was a book that only had a few readers, and those happened to be the DNFers?

Even average books have an audience out there, and finding those readers (often by writing more, then retconning that audience backwards) is easier than endlessly revising a book towards some misguided sense of better that doesn't really exist.

If you have not yet published (well, aren't you brave for being three books deep into a series where I assume you have been? I'm impressed!), then hopefully all of this is just background context for you to consider as you plan your next steps. Please remember that I don't regret any of my publishing steps. They all brought me to this moment right now, and right now is exactly where I need to be to move forward in the direction I want to go.

---

1. I really do want to stress that both WLW content and rom coms about SEALs are saleable products. They weren't monetizable by me because I didn't have a framework set up to capture those readers, and the readers I had previously retained from my other work saw those stories as too

different from what I'd previously written. If I wanted to commit to writing those, I'd need to do a hard restart.

2. Did Not Finish; I'm a serial DNFer, life is too short to read books that you don't love, and there's no explaining the alchemy; no shame to the DNF, I love it! But I don't always understand it when it's someone else's miss.

CHAPTER 7
CATALOGUE ASSESSMENT

IN *ROMANCE YOUR PLAN*, I said, "brand is created in the marketplace; without that market response, it's simply an attempt at a brand."

The second step in getting to where you want to be as a writer, after naming your goals, is to analyze what you have already done on the path to get there.

Which means looking at everything you have written to date.

I call this a **catalogue assessment**.

And it's literally just writing down every book you've ever written, and some that you want to write, grouping them in lists.

It's hard to describe a tool that starts with a blank page. It's a bit of marketing magic, really, for me to tell you that writing things down on a piece of paper is a Great New Idea!

But here's a secret: most things start with a blank page. Sometimes people will create a basic outline for you, and shill that .pdf file to you as a way to get you onto their email list for authors, so they can sell you a course or something. But that basic outline isn't anything you can't sketch out yourself.

So instead of creating a template, I'm going to show you how I do it myself. What you want to do is sketch out all your books, linking ones that are similar, and separating those that are different.

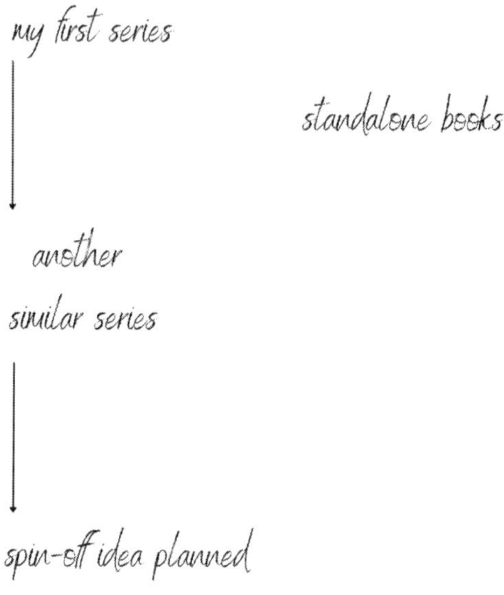

In the example above, I have suggested that you put similar series down the left hand side, and things that are different on the right, with anything very off-brand tucked away in the bottom corner. You can do this on paper, or you can do it in Canva, which is where I built these models. Here is one for my

Zoe series. (And you can see I did it just with series names, not individual book titles)

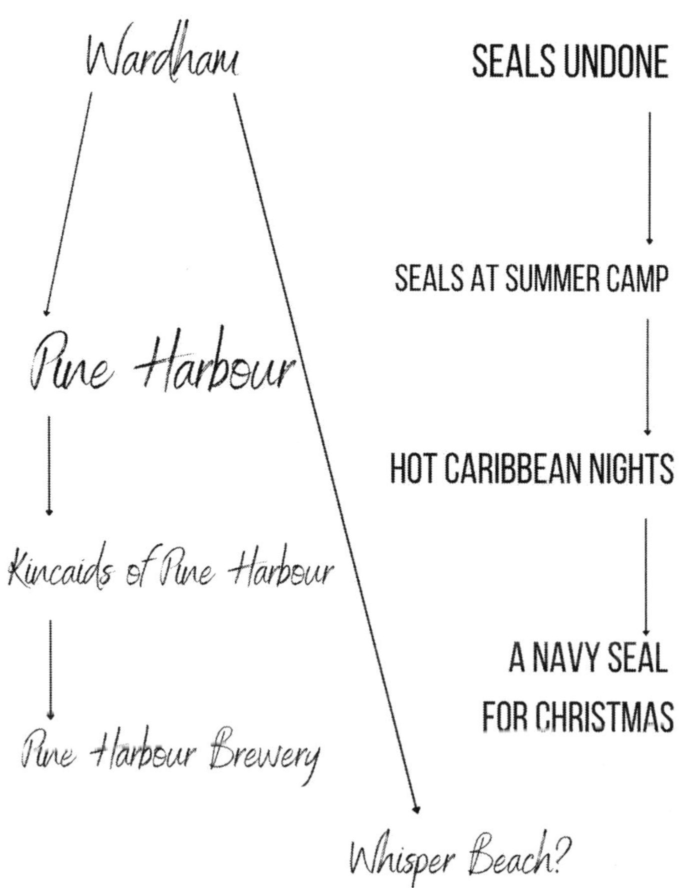

VIKINGS IN SPACE

That's not bad, right? You can see the progressive, cumulative catalogue growth, with one exception (Vikings in Space). I don't even have to label what the two main columns are. Well, here's my Ainsley catalogue.

~~Horus Group~~
erotic romantic suspense
renamed:
Forbidden Bodyguards

Frisky Beavers
erotic romance
with hockey

Billionaire Secrets
rom coms

Secrets and Lies duet
erotic romance

Off the Ice
high-heat hockey romance

wlw short stories
(new pen name?
Gigi Ford?)

It's a mess. And I started writing these books *after* my focused success in 2014! If there is any takeaway message from these two catalogue assessments, it is that any of us can go off the rails at any time.

And for what it is worth, Ainsley is the pen name I have hit the USA Today list with a full-price release; Zoe hasn't done that yet. Being organized has some serious benefits, especially when it comes to leveraging backlist for long-term financial stability, but it is not necessary for being a "successful author". What does Ainsley have going for her?

That's where I write the books that terrify me and thrill me in equal measure. Zoe's backlist is safe. Ainsley's front list is exciting.

See how those aren't loaded terms like *good* and *bad*? They both have utility.

CHAPTER 8

LET'S BUILD A PLAN TO GET THERE (A UNIQUELY YOU PLAN)

WHAT MOVES THE NEEDLE? And what IS the needle?

One of the objectives of this book is to help you develop some decision making tools. How do we choose which direction to go in? How can we align an action now to point in the direction of a goal down the road?

And first of all, how do we know what progress looks like?

The burning questions I have asked over the years are, what moves the needle? What attracts readers, and what retains them?

Those are the one-two punch of building a brand, as I see it. **Hooking new-to-me readers**, and **holding on to them**, which means, ideally, that after I've hooked them, they have opened my books and consumed them.

How do we get readers to open the books we have convinced them to buy? That's another burning question.

We can get fixated on the wrong things. What works for someone else doesn't appeal to us, we don't have the same enthusiasm for... insert anything here. A serialized story for newsletter subscribers, a drip automation campaign for email subscribers, re-targeting FB ads to people who have hit your website and been captured by a pixel, targeting cold audience readers via CPC ads, writing a long series with hooks between each books, writing trope-laden short novels, writing long, epic, angsty trilogies, writing quickly, rapid releases, long pre-order campaigns, slow build audiences with a five year plan.

Every single one of those ideas is genius.

And the one that you bristled at, the one you don't *like*, may not be genius for *you*, but then you should give it zero attention. It's a non-factor for you. Every ounce of energy you pour into disliking an idea is an ounce of energy you could have spent on something that you are enthusiastic about.

And here is where I admit that I am not speaking from on high. I can get gobbled up by the judgement monster as much as anyone else, and I'm susceptible to jealousy, too. Judgement and jealousy have been, at times, barriers to my success.

They aren't the only ones. The title of this book, Romance Your Goals, comes from the fact that I have a deep-seated fear around big dreams.

It shook loose when I attended RAM in 2019, but my relationship to understanding that fear began two years before that.

Four years ago, my husband had a breakdown. He was an infantry soldier, at the peak of his career in the military. We both worked—a lot—and then suddenly we were a family in crisis.

The trajectory of a career can change in an instant.

From May 2014 to November 2017, I was a perpetual motion machine of writing words and coming up with new book marketing ideas. Anything seemed possible.

And then suddenly the writing stopped. My life revolved around therapy appointments—his, multiple times a week. Mine. Ours.

A lot of walks, and late nights, and early mornings.

So much tea. All the love in the world, a lot of tears.

No writing.

Not for six months, and when I picked it back up again, the words that flowed weren't the words I used to write.

The spring of 2018 was the first time I really implemented the mid-range goal work I mentioned in chapter five. I took a tool I had been using for a few years (planning a year of marketing activities, which I outline in *Romance Your Plan*), and challenged myself to plan out a year without any releases.

Just in case.

And I had to really sit with that possibility. It was a clear example of my priorities suddenly shifting, and what that would mean for the plans I already had in place.

I DIVIDE the books I have written into before November 2017 and after May 2018. Those two catalogues may be invisible in difference to anyone else, but to me, there are clear demarcations when I look at them. I see all the books I had wanted to write before 2017, but didn't get to—and now I probably will never, because I am fundamentally not that person anymore. (This might not be the place to talk about grief, but sometimes we do need to grieve goals we have to let go of, in order to make room for new ones)

What I see when I look at these two different eras in my life are two distinctly different plans—and the books are a reflection of those two different plans.

In the end, I quite like this new plan, and where it is heading. But it took me longer than I like to admit to come to that sense of peace. I hope by sharing my journey, I can speed up that reconciliation for you, if you are ever in a similar position.

If a career can be rocked in an instant, it can be made in an instant as well, by making some radical changes that free you from what you don't want and point you in the direction of where you really *do* want to be. Maybe five years down the road, maybe one. How much radical change do you think you can make happen in the next 12 months?

It is hard work. It is commitment to a plan that is going to change. The commitment is not to the minutae, but to the overarching goal. To the framework.

Indeed, it can be a tactical error to get too tangled up in, "I promised my readers I would finish this series" or "I need to do X before I can start Y." But if Y serves your goal, and X does not, where does that obligation come from?

Fear, maybe.

If you want permission to do a hard reset on your plan, to better align your plan to your goals, I grant it. You don't need to get in your own way anymore.

So how do we get there? We build a wall. Or lay a path, depending on the analogy you prefer. Stone by stone, brick by brick. Or, (and don't feel badly if this is you), maybe pebble by pebble.

CHAPTER 9

BUILD A PLAN? BUILD A WALL

IN THIS CHAPTER and the next, I'm going to share a couple of different visual models of a framework for creating a chain of mid-range and short term goals that will nestle inside your long term goals.

I picture the next five years of my career as a garden wall, and mapping out the progression towards my major goal is sort of like reverse engineering how the wall was built. What does it look like when I finish? Each brick or stone represents a decision I will make between now and when the wall is finished: a product I will create or a platform plank I will develop.

And there are a *lot* of different ways to build a wall. (I also will share a pyramid analogy later on, if you're not sure about this wall image)

The key takeaway here is to build a list of achievable mile markers that point you in the right direction.

For me, the tools are:

- Mission/vision/priorities stated clearly as the foundation

- Chunkable pieces that can shift around (embracing the moving parts of a successful business)
- strong products
- efficient production team
- robust distribution channels
- Progressive, consecutive content
- Long term plan (so we can visualize what the wall will look like when finished)

My wall is going to look different from yours, but a general note: the size of your bricks may vary, but most of us are not serving up boulders every single time. A lot of my early lessons about publishing were around unpacking myths that most of publishing is about Big Successes, when really writing genre fiction is a wild careen from projects of various sizes to more projects of other sizes, in an endless, bumpy ride…

The size of your bricks do not determine whether or not you'll build a wall: they only determine how many bricks it will take to get the job done.

Every time you start over again, you are back to digging a trench and laying a foundation. And then, ahead of you, is still the brick-by-brick task of creating product and building a platform.

So when you pivot to a new plan—which I have done, and fully support—do it with a clear assessment of the partially built wall you are stepping away from, and the building materials you plan to use on the new wall.

Some people build walls out of boulders. Only a few significant pieces, but they take strength, patience, and significant investment of time and/or money to properly source. (When thinking about goal profiles, these are the **outliers**!) Others prefer pebbles, which are readily available and easily sourced all by yourself. In between, there are bricks and stones of all shapes and sizes.

One of the hardest parts of developing my own author career has been realizing that at times, I've been focused more on modelling my wall after someone else's ideal design, and not my own. This is why I like to think about that five year question, **what do *I* want to have written?** Centre yourself in the design of your plan. Throughout your career, *you* will be the only constant.

What does this look like?

A foundational platform of honest priorities, and a clear enthusiasm for where you want to go (see chapters three, four, and five): your goal is the capstone of your wall, and in between the foundation and that capstone are however many [bricks, stones, pebbles, boulders] it takes to get it as high as you want it to be.[1]

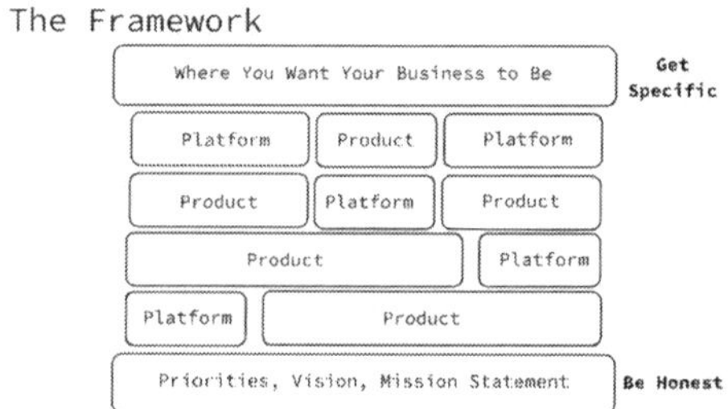

What are those building blocks? They are alternating pieces of product and platform.

There are two ways to think of **product**, as different brand elements (like a series or world), or different revenue streams (ebooks, audio, translations, etc.). Some people produce a lot of product (me!), others focus on making each brick in their wall as large (significant) as possible.

Platforms are how we connect with readers. Retailers, market partners like BookBub, our own website, email lists, and our brand presence on social media. Everyone will have a different combination of platforms that they gravitate towards, and I'm agnostic about the value of any of them. That value comes from how you engage with them. Does Tiktok sell books? Sure, yes, definitely, and not always are all correct answers. It really depends on you.

I'm going to share some examples now of how this looked for me from 2014-2017, and from 2019-2023.

In May 2014, I set an *initial goal* of replacing my full-time income from working at the university. At some point, that morphed or developed into a loftier $10k/month long-term consistency goal.

(Goals aren't supposed to be easily achieved. If they were that, they would simply be tasks.)

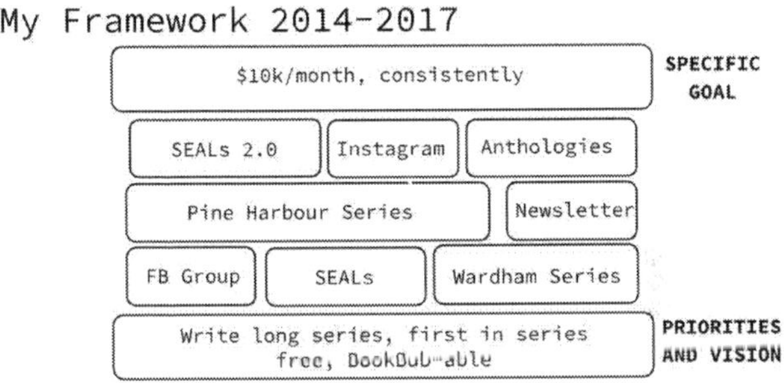

Prior to being laid off, my goal/capstone target was...write books? Release books in a series? It's hard for me to remember, exactly. But it was *not* income oriented. As soon as my life circumstances shifted, and my goal crystallized, more of the bricks that would be required to build this wall became clear. (More on this in the next chapter).

What I want to show first, though, before we get to the

progression of actually *building/doing*, is how my goal changed between 2017 and 2019.

But before I share the next framework plan, I want to talk about 2018 a bit more.

The year outside the plan. The year where my only plan was monthly marketing of my backlist, i.e. solely short term goals like "keep this business afloat" and "try to stay a few months ahead but have grace when that doesn't happen".

2018 was the first year after 2014 that I didn't hit the income goals I had set for myself. I stopped building that wall, couldn't build any further… and my income plummeted. (That will happen if you don't release anything, don't send any emails, don't go on social media for months!)

But by the summer, I had a backlist marketing plan in place, and my income stabilized at a lower but manageable and workable level. A new baseline.

I promise I'm not glossing over doing the work. Those details will come later. Right now we're just talking about mapping out the plan! And my point here is, in 2018, I paused the Master Plan, and went for an Interim Plan instead. I needed a period of pause.

There is a lot to be said for rest. It allows for recovery and reflection. I remember when my kids were little, their sleep would often be disrupted before a major milestone like learning how to walk and talk.

Before we can do something consciously, our subconscious needs to prepare itself. We need to try, and fail, and process, and think, and figure out how to try again, differently. We can't force that cycle.

So while I have been a full-time author since 2014, most of the income I made in 2018 was carrying forward from the success of the years before that. It was an important lesson: there will be lean years, not just financially, but also emotionally and creatively. The more we conserve during flush years, the better prepared we will be to weather those down turns in our productivity.

We cannot avoid the fallow period. We can only prepare for it, and then wait.

Or, while waiting, do some mindful rest and reflection! I did a *lot* of professional development between 2018 and 2020.

And one of those efforts was Holly Darling's Business Mastermind for Authors. Part bootcamp, part course, part cohort-of-artists, this mastermind was mostly about business structure.

And a part of a solid business plan is a mission and vision statement. This was not news to me—because I'd passed that same advice on to other authors myself!—but the depths to which Holly pushed me to revise my mission statement were deeper than what i could push myself to.

She challenged me on my *why*, and *for whom* I was writing. It took a month to agonize over bullet-point lists and big questions. But when I finished, I had a lofty statement to use as a touchstone for every major decision I wanted to make over the next five years.

> My mission is to create bestselling stories that reflect my readers' dreams, and that inspire them to foster more meaningful relationships and strive for a better community. My books are hopeful, heartwarming, idealistic, sexy, and earnestly real about what holds us back from reaching the next level. My readers get attached to my fully-realized characters and memorable settings full of hope and heat.

This mission statement was crafted out of classes with Holly Darling and Becca Syme (Write Better Faster)

We know what to do, but it's normal to need to brainstorm and workshop with smart peers and trusted experts. The most important word I added to this mission statement was a late addition, too.

Bestselling.

But when it came time to build a new framework, that was the word I put at the foundation again.

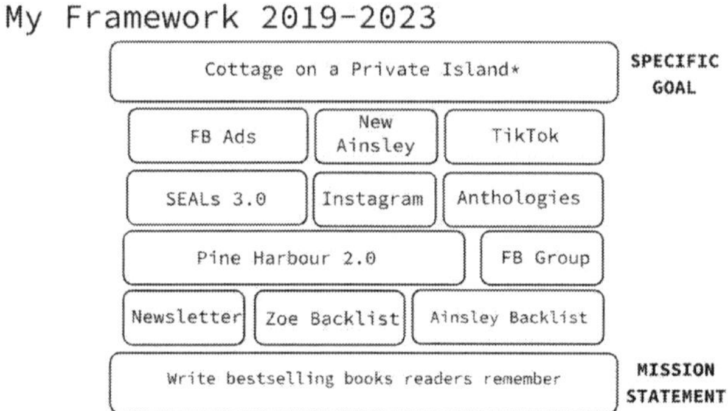

The "cottage on a private island" goal is a bit of hyperbole, more representative than literal. But I want more than the aggressive monthly income goal from before. I want to free myself from the income stability I sought in the years after leaving my full-time job, and be more open to periods of intense highs and frustrating lows. I know I can weather them now, and I know how to plan for a rebound success.

Now it's your turn to build some blueprints. In the next chapter, I'll show you *all* the possible bricks I can imagine, and you can start sketching out options.

How do you put this theory into action?

Use the framework. At the bottom, scribble your mission statement, or a top priority. Something to remind you of why you are doing this. At the top, write a goal. Make it a big one, not something you can easily achieve. Something that you will need to work for quite a while to accomplish.

And in between start layering in what you have already done. Then, use the pyramid in the next chapter (and spelled out in list form in chapter 18) to find adjacent blocks that excite you. Be mindful that you have a reasonable balance of product and platform, although it does not need to be 50-50. Your right ratio may be different from mine.

---

1. If the charts in this chapter are too small to read, you can find them on my website, and larger copies of all diagrams you need are included in the Appendix at the back of the paperback edition

CHAPTER 10

ZOE'S HIERARCHY OF PUBLISHING NEEDS

GENERALLY SPEAKING, publishing success is most evenly found once we figure out a plan that delivers us progressive, consecutive growth in the metrics we care about.

For some, that will be primarily income. But for others, reader retention numbers are just as valuable. (In the next chapter, I will dig deeper into the metrics that I started to track in 2018, and why I think non-sales metrics are hugely important as predictors of success.)

That being said, I can't think of any author who *only* has progressive, consecutive growth. It is normal for books to hit the market in variable ways. There are too many factors, most of them out of our control, to have all of them work out in favour even most of the time.

(Aaron Sorkin points out in one of his Masterclass lessons that writers hold themselves to impossibly high standards for success. Professional baseball players who miss two out of every three times at bat are Hall of Fame material, after all.)

The next three pages are another visual representation of career growth. Instead of a wall, representing a slice of a career, instead let's look at the totality of my career to date:

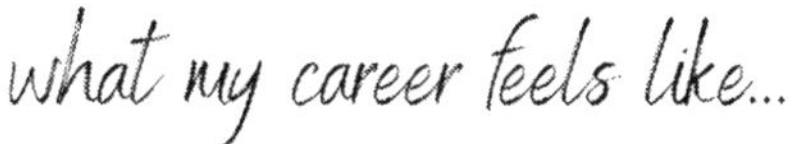

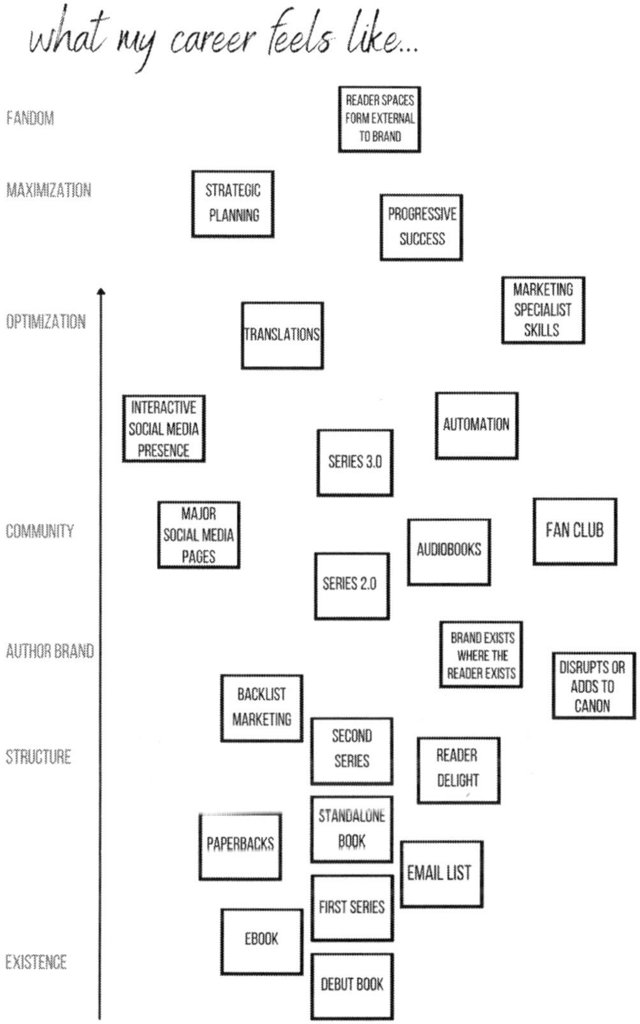
what my career feels like...
FANDOM
MAXIMIZATION
OPTIMIZATION
COMMUNITY
AUTHOR BRAND
STRUCTURE
EXISTENCE
READER SPACES FORM EXTERNAL TO BRAND
STRATEGIC PLANNING
PROGRESSIVE SUCCESS
MARKETING SPECIALIST SKILLS
TRANSLATIONS
INTERACTIVE SOCIAL MEDIA PRESENCE
AUTOMATION
SERIES 3.0
MAJOR SOCIAL MEDIA PAGES
AUDIOBOOKS
FAN CLUB
SERIES 2.0
BRAND EXISTS WHERE THE READER EXISTS
DISRUPTS OR ADDS TO CANON
BACKLIST MARKETING
SECOND SERIES
READER DELIGHT
PAPERBACKS
STANDALONE BOOK
EMAIL LIST
FIRST SERIES
EBOOK
DEBUT BOOK

I labelled this scatter chart after the fact with some tiers of what I call the Hierarchy of Publishing Needs: Existence, Structure, Author Brand, Community, Optimization, Maximization, and Fandom.

This is a riff on Maslow's hierarchy of needs, and if I reorganize these building blocks into a pyramid, it looks like this:

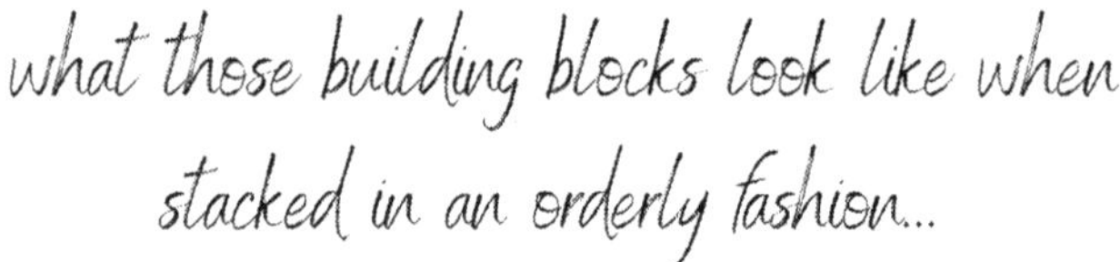

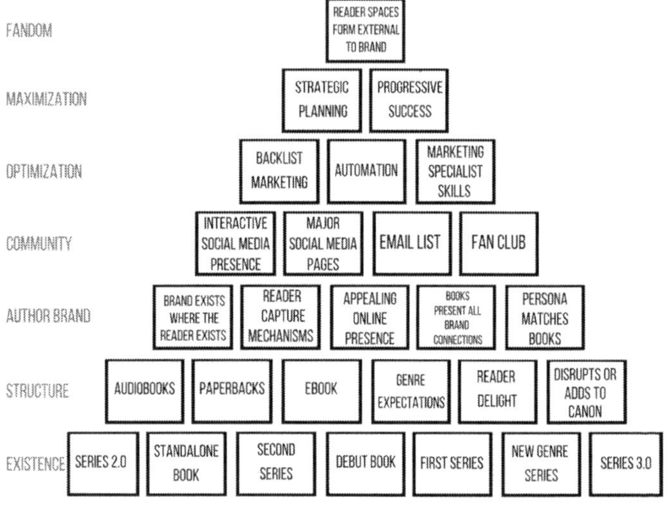

This a big, broad pyramid with all the possible blocks I can think of included (see chapter 18 for these blocks in list form). This is what a mature indie author's career might look like after a decade or more of investment and building. This is not a to-do list! This is a stack of things to goal towards, and consider as options when planning your first wall. (see chapter 14, Case Study #2, for examples of how I put this into action with my secret alter-ego in 2021)

And while the bottom layers are required for the layers

above them to happen, this is not a single, smooth upward trajectory plan. In fact, the path I took—even when simplified into a graphic, looks like someone taped a GPS device to a toddler and then encouraged them to chase a cat around a house.

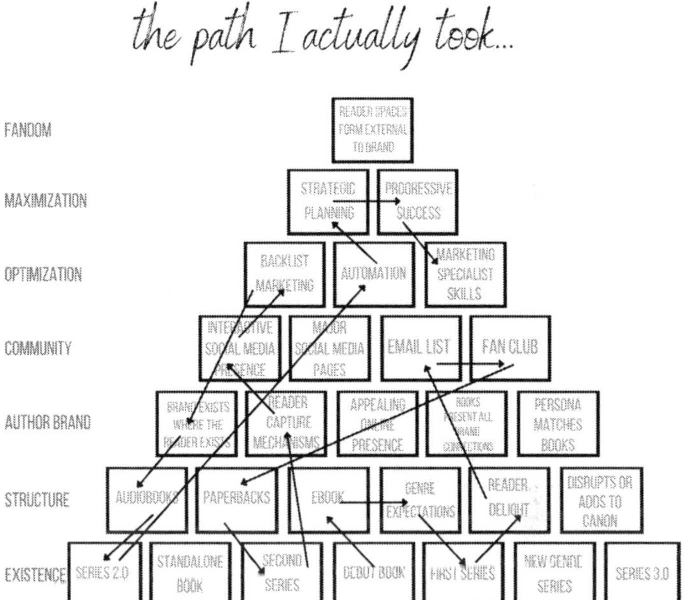

And you can see blocks I still haven't touched on yet!

For a more robust examination of the options to include inside a marketing plan for a year, go back to *Romance Your Plan*. And once you have a sketch of a wall, or a path, or a pyramid you might want to build, turn the page and we can discuss what metrics you can track as to see progress.

CHAPTER 11

METRICS MATTER

LEARN HOW TO MEASURE SUCCESS BEYOND SALES

WHEN I PUBLISHED my first book, I sold sixty copies of it in my first month (mostly to friends and family). And then sales slowed, and stopped.

I released my next book, and then my third. Sales rebounded with each release, then slumped again.

There's something about sales that invite comparison. Even if not with other authors (always dangerous), we can't help but compare against ourselves, month to month and even day to day.

Other metrics more naturally lend themselves to only viewing in a cumulative way.

Newsletter subscribers and new fan club members.

Words written. Words published.

The day I was laid off, I had 238,000 words published across 6 titles (3 novels, 1 short story, 2 novellas), written in just over two years (and published in eleven months).

By December of that year, I **added** 275,000 words in seven months, bringing my career word count published total to 513,000 words in a year and a half.

In seven months, I more than doubled how many novels I

had for sale, and went from one series to three series. And it took almost all seven months for the income to catch up to that surge in productivity.

Non-sales metrics kept me going that whole time.

From January 2015 to November 2017—in hindsight, a small period of time that felt like a glorious lifetime—I wrote consistently and made a lot of money doing it. By the end of 2015, I passed the million words published mark (498,000 words published in 2015). In 2016 and 2017 I wrote a combined 977,000 words (466,000 and 511,000).

I hit the 2 million word published mark right before my life came to a crashing halt.

In January 2018, I realized my income was going to dip below that threshold I'd passed three years earlier—for the first time, I was going to earn less in a month than I had in my day job. It didn't matter if it happened once, or even a few times over the next little while, because I had saved most of my earnings to that point. (I will always be grateful to my past self for buying a used Ford Escape instead of a Land Rover; the price difference bought me six months of not looking at my business.)

So right now, if you want to scribble down a depressing takeaway note from this part of the book: save your money. There will be times in the future when you don't make as much as you do now, and future you will be grateful for the stockpile.

In 2018, I wrote 186,000 words, more than half of them in a single novel. I published 211,000 words, because I'd started writing ahead the year before.

In 2019, I published 213,000 words. In 2020, 215,000 words, and I worried this was my new pace for life. I worried, but I also took some comfort in my new plateau. It was, at least, consistent.

But other things happened over those three years: I started to give away more books, and actively grow my newsletter. I wrote bonus content for readers, at first sporadically, and last year, more consistently. And then I started a secret pen name.

All of those non-sales metrics helped make 2021 a much better year then expected, mostly reflected in an unexpected word count total for the year of 328,655 published words. (This count is more precise than the others because I kept track as I released each book.)

	2013	2014	2015	2016	2017	2018	2019	2020	2021
WORDS PUBLISHED (ANNUAL)	122,000	391,000	498,000	466,000	**511,000**	*211,000*	213,000	215,000	328,655
NEW BOOKS PUBLISHED	3	8	13	**13**	*11*	*6*	*4*	*5*	*7*
SERIES WITH FREE BOOKS AVAILABLE	1 (NOVELLA)	1	3	4	5	6	8	8	8
BONUS WORDS WRITTEN						5000	5000	5000	25,000
ZOE NEWSLETTER	652	1854	6798	11,002	14,882	21,733	32,618	39,781	44,381
AINSLEY NEWSLETTER			2236	4286	8074	**9929**	*9516*	*9152*	*12,532*
SECRET ALTER EGO NEWSLETTER									*1500*

If this chart is too small to read, you can find it on my website:

www.romanceyourbrand.com/romance-your-goals/

I highly recommend building a chart like this, focused on the non-sales metrics you are growing. Celebrate the mile markers along the way. Make sure you have enough of these and they aren't all income or sales focused.

Why do I press this point? Because if we don't have mile markers that will tell us that we're on the right track before the income starts to lift, we might falter. There are many points in our career when this can happen. Right out of the gate, but also if we hit a period of stagnation.

Sometimes, it feels like we aren't moving forwards. Sometimes, it feels like we're moving backwards. So we pivot, we reinvent ourselves, we start over. Again and again.

I have done this a few times. But it is my saving grace that more often than not, I have stuck the course.

The decisions we make in the moment, about the moment, are often emotional. The plans we made, the goals we set three, six, or twelve months ago—those are probably safer to trust.

(But I need proof they work, Zoe.)
(The proof is down the road, I'm sorry, stick with it.)

Intermediate goals. Non-sales metrics. These are what I go to when I'm feeling weak and unsure about the plan.

And brand growth takes time! It happens in layers and requires a solid infrastructure that doesn't always pay off right away. Another reason why we need to track our own metrics and not just rely on what others tell us to do: what works for others might not work for us (yet) because they have the infrastructure in place and we don't. Put the infrastructure in place and focus on production (this means writing, and writing well), and the rest will fall into place in good time.

LEVELLING UP

"You need to niche down to rich up." I think I've heard a variation on that sentiment more times in the last year than ever before. And I always want to make the counter argument: don't rush to niche. You'll know when it's time.

(You might know. You might not, and no advice is universal. But whew, not everyone needs to find a niche right away.)

The flip side of the whole "focus on one thing" advice is that sometimes we need to write a few different things before we really settle into a groove—I certainly did! Someone on

Tiktok[1] described it as a capital letter T model. You go back and forth on the top line, creating different things, and then at some point, you'll figure out where the centre of your business should be, and that's where you start to drill down.

I don't even think one long series is that vertical centre line; I see the top horizontal line as a collection of series, stand-alones, and collaborative projects. The vertical line is the twenty year career that evolves after you finish the genre exploration.

For some of us, it'll be a gut call. This is it, this is where I want to stay and create a while. But for others, we might need metrics to reveal what is right in front of us.

---

1. I really did try to find out who to attribute this to, but TikTok isn't helpful in that regard, and I couldn't find anything similar in a Google search. If you are a TikTok viewer and you ever see a video of a middle-aged man talking about this business model, send it to me and I'll provide all the credit to him.

CHAPTER 12

THE SAGA OF THE GENRE FICTION AUTHOR

ONE OF THE hardest realizations for me to accept for myself, even as I counselled my peers to embrace the journey, is just how many steps there are *after* you start to embrace your Big Scary Hairy Goal. (And also, how many stages of your career you might go through before you're willing to name it at all!)

There is a whole process for unpacking what stands between you and success, and then a whole other process to building the scaffolding that will protect that success once you embark on that next stage of the journey.

Plus, you're going to rinse and repeat that cycle a bunch of times as you level up, plateau, level up again, plateau again...

It's a lot.

Except that's the gig.

Nobody ever said that writing wasn't *work*.

I sketched this out in bullet point form, like I did a lot of the other chapters in this book. And then I decided that no, it was better left as a free form list with limited explanation.

This is how I see the Saga of the Genre Fiction Author, a dramatic story told in thirteen acts.

Pre-publication: I just want to WRITE

First [year, series, few titles]

This is starting to feel like a brand, maybe?

The marketing machine actually feels like it's starting to work

"all the things go wrong... PIVOT"

FEEL FEEL FEEL, So much is a gut call

Oh crap, a plateau

Big Scary Hairy Goal

"all the things go wrong... PIVOT AGAIN"

Barriers to next level success

Boundaries to protect next level success

It's an evolution, baby

Always be goalling

Your goals *will* change. More often than you think. And finding progressive growth in your career will be tied to how willing you are to pivot just enough, point yourself in that new direction, and stretch to meet that new goal, without abandoning cumulative successes (even if nascent!) you've had to date.

There isn't one thing that will make a difference. And there will be many "one things" that you are sure are not helpful, based on limited data! But years later, you may look back and think, oh. That helped after all.

BRAND MATURITY

I think we've all heard the maxim, don't compare your WIP (work in progress) to someone else's finished project. This is true for books, and lives—Pinterest and Instagram aren't real, for example—but it's also true for businesses.

Author brands evolve over time, and then they appear really slick online, that's evidence of brand maturity. At that point, it's harder to see how they got there, but it's not impossible. If you're really impressed by someone's Instagram engagement and posting style, for example, scroll WAY back on their feed. Check out their growth. Same with Facebook or YouTube, you can go back and see much earlier content, and if you scroll fast, or search for a much older time period, you'll see a stark difference rather than the slow, seamless growth that happened over time.

(If you don't see that evolution, if they were slick from day one, then that's not a first pen name, and you can assume they did all the hard work under a different brand.)

EMBRACE THE LONG TAIL

The ground work that you lay now will pay off down the road. It takes a monumental amount of effort to make small changes *right now*, but small efforts right now can make monumental change *later*.

Nothing illustrates this point more clearly than a decision I made in December 2014 to ask a few author friends if they wanted to collaborate on a free book promotion idea. What turned into "ZoeBub" is the first of three case studies I'll share as examples of goal-oriented plans in action.

CHAPTER 13

CASE STUDY #1: BUILDING A CROSS PROMOTION COMMUNITY

IN DECEMBER 2014, I was coming to the end of my severance package. I'd written a heck of a lot of words in the seven months since being laid off. I'd done a couple of promo pushes on my free books, and seen a direct ROI (return on investment) from that effort, but felt like I'd exhausted the reputable paid promotion sites.

I bought a website domain that sounded like it might host book events, added it to my shared hosting account, and put the feelers out. Would anyone like to do a group free book blast? A simple list, we all share it to our newsletters on the same day. Try to use our collective strength to get a visibility boost, and give our readers a nice, no-strings-attached gift the day after Christmas.

On Boxing Day, December 26, 2014, we had our first "Stuff Your Kindle" event.

Thirty-seven authors joined the first promo. There were fifty-two authors involved when we did it again in February 2015. That participation level held steady for the next year, and grew in a linear way until word of mouth and the reputation of the event hit a sweet point in 2017, and invites to the group started to jump after each quarterly event.

Today, the group has more than 1000 members and more than 400 authors regularly participate in any given event. Last year I had to move our website to a more expensive hosting site, because we were generating traffic in excess of 6000 visitors per hour.

A small action in December 2014 has directly led to more than 25,000 downloads of just my books over the years. It set into motion a chain of events that built networking relationships, and found readers for my non-fiction, and gave me confidence to shout from the rooftops that enthusiasm and community buy-in are just as valuable as paying cold hard cash for promotion.

Maybe even more valuable, because if you build a vehicle that you can point towards goals, you can take it in a variety of directions. (Over the years, we have tried other cross promo under the same banner; I return to the free book blast, though, because it's most universally appreciated and understood by readers.)

What is the takeaway lesson? There is compound interest earned on nurturing good ideas.

CHAPTER 14

CASE STUDY #2: STARTING (OVER) FROM SCRATCH

"ZOE, it was different in 2013. Easier to get started. Easier to find an audience."

I hear this a lot. It didn't feel right, but I didn't have any data to counter those arguments. Didn't, past tense, because now I do.

In May 2021, I started a secret pen name. I went through all the steps I would recommend to anyone starting out. I secured the online presence for my author brand, wrote a good book that would meet genre expectations, hired a decent editor at a reasonable price, and came up with a release plan that looked a lot like the orderly fashion pyramid I shared in chapter 10.

All I needed was a PR company to help me spread the word about the book, because I didn't want to use my Zoe/Ainsley platform at all. I emailed four companies that work with indie authors; three of them were companies I had worked with as Zoe.

But I wasn't emailing them as Zoe, I was emailing them as Alter-Ego (mostly for the data; what was it like to start as a debut author in 2021?).

And only one company emailed me back. But they were

happy to take my money in exchange for their service, and we were off to the races.

(For the record, I had a lot of people not return my emails as Zoe back in 2013, too. This didn't feel harder than it had back then, but it was a reminder to me that it *is* hard to get started!)

My first book was a novella; this is advice I took from myself, which is an admitted advantage. They are faster and cheaper to produce. I spent $150 on the release promotion, which felt like a splurge (trading money for some saved time, to get those first reviews and a bit of visibility to the usual suspects in book review spaces). I spent $240 on editing, and I did the cover and formatting myself. To be fair, let's assign those with market price values of $120 (what I recently paid for a premade cover for another project) and $60 (what I would charge myself for formatting). Oh, and the website and email: $100 for the first year.

I decided to go with MailerLite for my newsletter, because it would be free for the first 1000 subscribers.

And I wrote a bonus scene for that book, for newsletter subscribers only, so anyone who did read it would have a clear Call To Action (CTA) at the back of the book to get on my email list.

Total launch cost: $670, and $150 of that was definitely optional. I don't think the PR company is necessary, and I could have achieved the same exposure by individually contacting bloggers and bookstagram/BookTok reviewers who are open to ARC offers.

I earned all of that back in the first month.

I released two more books by the end of the year, and in December, my newsletter list crossed the 1000 subscriber mark. Alter-Ego's email list is growing almost as fast as my Zoe email list, which has a lot more books pointed towards.

What is the big difference? I started this name with a

clear, single-minded intention. To write one kind of book, very well, and deliver more of the same to a targeted reader.

If you have considered starting over, but hesitated because it was hard before and you worry it might be harder now, please know that's not a universal experience.

I can't say for sure that it's *not* harder to start now, for the first time, compared to 2013. But I do know that it is much easier to start over, with the strength of nine years of knowledge driving choices, than it was to publish for the very first time.

CHAPTER 15

CASE STUDY #3: HARD PIVOT INTO AN UNEXPECTED SERIES 2.0

ON THE OTHER HAND, what about people who are stubbornly attached to what they have done before? Especially when some of those accomplishments *should* mean something still today?

Should.

Such an unhelpful word.

Meet my first alter-ego, Ainsley Booth. Three-time USA Today bestselling author, all for single title books. Of my three pen names, she has the most followers on Goodreads. "She" is also responsible for my two most widely distributed books of all time, *Prime Minister* and *Hate F*@k.*

And the bitch cannot sell a book to save her life right now. Welcome to the case study of a slump!

If you read chapter 7 about catalogue assessments, you probably won't be surprised to find out that I haven't found progressive, consecutive growth with my Ainsley books. Each series has been like starting over again, even among the ones that are sort of similarly themed.

By the fall of 2021, I had come to an understanding of my work under this pen name: I hadn't found "it" yet. If you read the levelling up section at the end of chapter 11 (Metrics

Matter), the random guy I saw on TikTok who talked about the T model of finding out where to niche? That analogy worked for me because it resonated deeply with my two very different experiences with brand.

Zoe has it, and Ainsley doesn't.

Key takeaway here: brand maturity is separate from individual book success!

So there I was on TikTok, scrolling, thinking about that guy's video and how I should have saved it, because what he described was *me to a T* (ha, the irony), and suddenly I found myself watching a hockey video.

Specifically, a video produced by the social media team of the Columbus Blue Jackets, documenting what time the different hockey players arrived at the rink before a game.

I was transfixed. I watched it three times, and sent it to a couple of friends. All those different players, with their different suits, and accessories: some with ear buds in, ignoring the camera, others giving a friendly wave; some arriving early, others squeaking in at the last minute; some dressed conservatively, others taking as much liberty as they could inside the dress code of a Nice Suit.

They were all characters in a book. A series laid itself in front of me, a group of different heroes just begging to be written about.

(For legal reasons, obviously this was just inspiration, and my books are not going to be fanfic about any real NHL team)

But I don't write hockey romance. Would it be another scribble along that top line of the letter T? I don't even know that much about hockey, despite being raised in small town Ontario, and having a kid who plays ball hockey, and having written a series about a prime minister who loves hockey.

A series that has a (pick up) hockey team at its core…

Well. *Fuck my life.*

Frisky Beavers was a hockey romance series all along. (If you're surprised at this realization, because you read chapter 7 and I call it a hockey romance there, that's new. I never, ever used that language before this realization. The Off The Ice series I have on the Ainsley catalogue assessment sketch is this series I'm talking about in this case study, too. It is what I'm going to write in 2022.)

Depending on how I write the final Frisky Beavers book, Off The Ice actually could be a strong Series 2.0 (see chapter 21) post-Frisky Beavers. Given that I'm publishing this book before I see this plan out, you'll be able to watch this case study unfold in real time. I don't know if my instinct here is correct, but I'm excited about this new series in a way I haven't been excited about any book in quite a while. It will be a good test of the hypothesis that enthusiasm is one of the most important factors in a book's success.

I haven't said it for a while, so let's go back to this: I'm no expert at any of this. I'm a peer on this journey. I'm still figuring stuff out, like *what is my brand* and *what should I write next* and *am I even good enough to write that.*

Your brand will evolve in the marketplace.

Be open to writing something unexpected next.

Yes, you are good enough to write that.

CHAPTER 16

GATHER THE TOOLS AND THE TEAM THAT WILL HELP YOU GET THERE

THE DEFINITION of frustration is doing the same thing over and over again and expecting a different result.

If you haven't yet achieved your goals, and you don't feel progressive, cumulative momentum in that direction—if, in fact, you feel a sinking feeling that you're going backwards—then you need to do something new.

Something has to change. But *what* that something is, that's entirely up to you.

This can be a real pain point for people who work hard. If you are working hard and not achieving your goals, I want to pause here and acknowledge that effort. I've talked to people who have written thirty books, because someone promised them that was the key to making full time income, but they are still struggling. And there have been times where, in short hand, the person making that promise may have been me.

There is no magic answer to making it.

But there are so many factors that encourage inertia. More than the number of levers it often feels like we could pull, maybe, in order to see change. And we can't pull them all, and it takes a lot objectivity, knowledge, and experience to best-guess which lever will make the biggest difference on any individual's catalogue of work.

So we often do nothing, and wait for a bolt of lightning.

THERE ARE four things we could do instead of waiting for a bolt of lightning. (Well, there are dozens of things, but in broad strokes, they group into four major options)

- Write more
- Change lanes
- Up one's marketing game
- Recruit publishing partners

Writing a novel is difficult for the vast majority of people who do it. It's also, obviously, *very* hard for those people who never do it.

There are some people though, for whom productivity is a lever that they can pull over and over and over again. These people often have first careers as copywriters and as journalists. And when they pivot to writing fiction, that volume of output is something they have reached mastery at—just producing words.

For others, increasing productivity is something that is going to take a lot of effort and may only see minimal reward. Compared to anything else that you could do, for example, like increasing your marketing efforts, or writing *different* books.

And conversely, for some of you writing different books feels like an impossible ask. But spending time on advertising or changing the packaging on existing books, those are maybe more doable.

As I brainstormed this chapter, I made a master to-do list, to show you that none of us can do it all. And then that was overwhelming, so I wrote another chapter on baby steps, a one, two, three approach to just getting started in a different direction, just moving the needle a little bit.

I'm going to share both of those next. But first I want to say that in addition to grabbing these tools and figuring out what order to press levers in, sometimes we need to lean on others.

Writing is mythologized as a solitary effort. It doesn't need to be. And publishing *really* doesn't need to be. As your career advances, keep an open mind to collaboration and outsourcing. There are ways to do both that start as limited test runs, to make sure the project meets your business goals, before evolving into a wider ranging commitment.

In the next two chapters, I explore some of these options in greater detail. Not for the first time in this book, I'm going to ask you to keep an open mind, because what I don't do is outline a precise marketing plan. If you want that, I'd point you back to *Romance Your Plan*, but even there, I just encourage you to do it yourself. The best plan you ever have will be the one you build yourself.

CHAPTER 17

BABY STEPS

I ATTENDED an excellent workshop last year on how to use TikTok as an author, and there was a ton of excellent advice in it. (If you ever get a chance to see Ana Huang present on anything to do with brand or social media, make the time!)

But one bit of advice jumped out at me, because it skipped over a pain point. The advice was something like, even if you can't respond to all comments, try to engage with comments left in the first hour. This tells the algorithm that you're an active user of the platform and it doubles the number of comments left in the first hour, because replies count, too. (This is a deep paraphrase)

My problem? I don't get comments in the first hour.

So many excellent bits of advice are for down the road, once you've built up a catalogue of [videos, books, whatever the content is]. And some people intuitively go straight to analyzing ideal structure, so the content they produce *from the start* is landing in an optimized way.

Some of us need more practice at content production than others.

And while I generally believe that any investment can be solved with time *or* money, or most commonly a mix of the two, I'm not sure we can speed up the process of learning the craft: be it writing, or video content creation. We will learn this at our own pace, and sinking money into the problem doesn't help.

That's true for everyone.

It is *very* true for those who don't have much money to start with.

In the same way with Maslow's Hierarchy of Needs means you have to take care of some basic, foundational elements, so too with Zoe's Hierarchy of Publishing: you need books to exist before anything else can happen. Focus on slaying barriers to that, first and foremost. Write, write, write. But then you also need to be confident that the books you are creating are going to land well in the market (even a niche part of it) before you sink money you don't really have into the production process.

In the introduction of this book, I talked about how some of us have more good choices available to us because of privilege. Let's return to that now.

WHEN YOU DON'T HAVE GOOD CHOICES

When money is excruciatingly tight, or you are a marginalized author wanting to write stories that feel niche for the market.

Test the minimum viable product: write short. Write fast. Barter. Swap. Do it on a pen name, and do it dirty. No website, DIY covers. Basic. You can always upgrade later.

To some, this is sacrilege. For me, it was the first move that has had a very long tail. The first book I wrote back in 2013? I paid for a copy edit on that, and *that's it.* No paid PR company to help launch it; I meticulously compiled a list of Goodreads reviewers to approach with an Advance Review Copy (ARC). I made the cover using a stock photo I "bought" with free credits one of the stock photo sites sent me after I signed up for an account but didn't buy any credits immediately. I didn't even self-host my own website at first.

And it's a move I've made again, more than a few times, over the years. You cannot tell by looking at my catalogue which books have been these hustle books, and which I invested a lot more money in.

Get slick at masking the hustle.

Because there is always hustle, one way or another. There is hustle in waiting for the right project to be championed by the right agent and sold to the right editor. Don't let anyone tell you that's the superior track compared to a less gate-keepered hustle. It's just another track.

And once you realize that it's *all* hustle, and everyone is faking it in one way or another, then you might find some new confidence to go after whatever it is that you want: including that trad deal, if that's where your goal profile lands.

WHEN YOU AREN'T TAKING ADVANTAGE OF GOOD CHOICES

Because you feel like you can't. Like you aren't good enough.

Whew. I just took a deep breath. Maybe you did, too.

I know it's easy in 2022 to echo literally everyone on TikTok and say, "trauma response!", but…sometimes a duck is a duck.

And I wouldn't be the girl who survived the darkest winter ever in 2017/2018 if I didn't say, gently, that we've all been through some shit, and it can really get in the way of letting us believe in anything better.

This is where my book on finding your publishing career

veers into vent about how inaccessible mental health services are, but at the very least, get on TikTok and search for trauma responses. Some of it is overwrought, but some of it is produced by real mental health professionals and might just prove a little helpful.

CHAPTER 18

THE MASTER TO-DO LIST

WE ALL ONLY HAVE TWENTY-FOUR HOURS IN A DAY

A COMMON QUESTION I get is, "How can I get my book noticed?"

It's almost as common as, "Can you look at my marketing plan and tell me what's missing?"

The answers are, *I don't know,* and *no*. Not because I'm mean, but because the best person to answer those questions is *you.*

Sorry to be the bearer of bad news!

Except it's great news. It means that the power to answer those question does lie within you. In fact, I think you already know the answer, but it's muddied by the fact that you also see a lot of other options. And it's possible that you don't like most of them, so it's very hard to discern which ones you do like, or think would be worth trying.

For one thing, which ones to try and *in which order* is a deeply personal answer that requires intimate knowledge of your catalogue and book sales data. I cannot assess that from the outside looking at a marketing plan or a single day snapshot of your books on the retailers, although sometimes I do try for fun.

But what I can offer is as detailed a list as I can ever make, a master to-do list, so you aren't trying to build your own master list from scratch. Start here, and sort this list into "Could do this now", "Could do this later", "Would prefer never to do this", and "This could be outsourceable" piles.

I'm not saying all of these are *good* or *bad.* Remember, those words are loaded and unhelpful to our purpose! We care more about safe vs exciting, and bring your best "does it spark joy" assessment to every part of this list.

And this is also not a consecutive task list. You will work on these in layers. You'll want to consult a master list of ideas, either this one or one of your own construction, every time you review your plan. Is it time to add something new?

Final caution: It is very important to remember that you need to keep returning to "bringing books into existence", though. There is only so much you can build on top of a single book or a single series.

ZOE'S HIERACHY OF PUBLISHING NEEDS, IN LIST FORM

BRINGING BOOKS INTO EXISTENCE:

- Debut Book (ever, and also per pen name!)
- First Series
- Second Series
- Standalone Book
- New Genre Series
- Series 2.0[1]
- Standalone Book that is a Project 2.0
- Series 3.0 (very next level, I haven't done this yet)
- Collaborative Projects
- Serialized Works
- Novella series

- Cliffhanger (one big arc) series
- Trilogies inside a larger series

FOCUSING ON OR IMPROVING BOOK STRUCTURE PART 1, FORMAT:

- available in ebook
- available in paperback
- available in hardcover (especially library access here)
- available in audiobooks

FOCUSING ON OR IMPROVING BOOK STRUCTURE PART 2, CONTENT:

- Meets Genre Expectations
- Surpasses Genre Expectations, causes much Reader Delight
- Disrupts or Adds to Canon

BUILDING AUTHOR BRAND

- brand exists where the reader exists on **social media**
- brand exists where the reader exists in **email** spaces
- brand exists where the reader exists in **website** searches
- capture mechanisms exist in these spaces to retain readers
- Books present all brand connections (newsletter, social media, website)
- Appealing Online Presence[2]
- author persona matches books

COMMUNITY

- interactive social media presence
- all major social media pages are updated with book news
- email list is leveraged to foster community
- fan club / reader group is actively managed

OPTIMIZATION

- automation is built wherever possible
- marketing specialist skills are leveraged where possible
- backlist marketing is a rolling, consistent business plank

MAXIMIZATION

- strategic planning is conscious and strong
- progressive success is goalled towards and tracked

Eagle-eyed writers will notice that I've left off the fandom tier of the pyramid. "Reader Spaces Form External to Brand" is not something we can put on our to-do list. It's just something that happens, sometimes, because we've done as much of everything else as we can.

YOU MIGHT BE WONDERING why I haven't talked about my favourite f-word yet on this list (free). If it's a master to-do list, why isn't "make one of your books free" on it?

Because that's a totally different thing. In the interest of completeness, I'll round this master to-do list out with marketing ideas (because I love them), but when it goes to goal setting and planning, the bricks are product and platform, not individual marketing levers we can push. Those are *inside* the bricks. Those are the details. Those are the *how*, and the bricks are the *what*. Your goal? That's the *why*.

Everything should point in that direction.

WAYS TO USE FREE AS A MARKETING LEVER

- free first in series
- free prequel
- limited time free book later in a series
- exclusive free offers via similar author newsletters
- paid email promotion of a free books
- free multi-author boxed set (digital collection)
- free offer to newsletter subscribers on your website
- free offer to newsletter subscribers using ads on social media
- evergreen social media content (share regularly!)

WAYS TO USE PRICE DISCOUNTS AS A MARKETING LEVER

- price reduction on a single novel
- price reduction on every book in a series
- price reduction on a digital collection (boxed set) of your own books
- price reduction on a digital collection (boxed set) of books by multiple authors
- price reduction event through a book retailer platform[3] (either just your book, or multiple author event)

I started to make a list here called "ways to use social media as a marketing lever", but I don't think that's quite the right approach. Social media falls under brand identity and advertising, and the marketing lever isn't "use social media", but more about copywriting. Long form, short form, sales copy, evergreen book promo hooks, ad copy, cold audience hooks, warm audience relationship developing, education for new readers... As authors who write for a living, it's remarkable how resistant we are to copywriting as a skill we should always be doing professional development on. If you've just made the scowliest face at this paragraph, put "outsource copywriting" on your long-term to-do list. That can be a maximization level brick, once you have books making you money, and when pushed *at that point*, hiring a specialist with copywriting skills can have a clear positive ROI for your business.

If you've ever looked at an author and thought, "wow, she has really good social media game, I could never", try swapping in the word copywriting instead. "Wow, she really has good copywriting game." It demystifies what needs to go on your to-do list!

---

1. Series 2.0 gets a whole chapter later in the book, don't worry if you don't know what it is yet
2. I think I was a little extra snarky when I wrote this part of the pyramid, but I'm leaving it in, with all caps on the Appealing Online Presence; I probably don't have that half the time, and that's fine. But I can see how that would be exciting for some people, and readers generally react well to nice things, and nice people. We can't all be that. Feel free to interpret this however you want, and remember that "appealing" is to your target audience, your fans, not to anyone you don't want to be appealing to.
3. I hesitate to put specific instructions on how to do this in a book because things change over time, but all the platforms have options here. Google Play has a promo price change tool that makes the discount visible on the book page; Kobo Writing Life has a Promotions tab on the author dashboard with regular monthly opportunities; Apple Books has an email list authors can request to be on for promotional opportunities, and authors who use Draft2Digital as a distributor to get to Apple Books have access to

this as well through D2D; Nook Press encourages marketing coordination as well; Amazon KDP has free and 99 cent countdown options for KDP Select authors. Some of these may change over time but they are accurate at the time of printing.

CHAPTER 19

HOW TO BELIEVE IN YOURSELF (OR FAKE IT TIL YOU BAKE IT IN)

I'M FEELING some anxiety about not giving enough of a detailed answer in the last chapter on What You Should Do, even after I spell out why I can't be the one to do that.

Doubt, she is a punishing bully.

How do you convince yourself you're the real deal, worthy of the hype and a top-tier plan? That's a million dollar question.

"Why do you think your book boxes won't have value?" This was a question my therapist asked me, in October, after I confessed to her that I have the supplies to make limited run book boxes for my readers sitting in my living room, and I have had them since last February.

I've been thinking about book boxes (mailed out bundles of paperbacks and related swag) for a year longer than I've had the supplies.

And yet, at the time of writing this chapter, I haven't done anything with any of it.

There will be some very good ideas in this book that you might want to do, and yet you tell yourself that you cannot.

There are very good ideas out there in the wider world that *I* want to do, earnestly, and yet I tell myself I cannot.

I'm reminded of coaches in high school telling me that I need a Can Do mentality, not a Can't Do attitude. I'm pretty sure the personal trainer I had for five years said something similar. All you have to do is tell yourself you can, and then you can.

To which I say, bullshit.

Except of course, there's a kernel of truth to that. Not that everyone can do a minute-long plank, of course. But that if you want to do a minute-long plank, you need to *start* by telling yourself you can.

If you start with the idea that you can't, you've made the next steps so much harder, maybe even impossible.

This is true for any goal.

I want to send out book boxes. That's a goal I have. And after I say it, if I'm very quiet and sit with my thoughts, I hear a lot of whispers in my head.

What if people don't like them? What if they aren't a good value? You should have sprung for the pretty custom boxes, nobody wants a white cardboard box. Those books are old now, it would have been better as a new release event. Maybe you should wait and do it for another book. Maybe just don't do it at all.

This level of self-doubt feels unusual for me. I'm a pretty confident person, as evidenced by all the books and the non-fiction books and the glorious smile I plaster all over social media.

But we're all human.

If your self-doubt ever feels lonely, please know that I also struggle with that negative self-talk that gets in the way of setting a progress path toward my stated goal.

I bet you're already yelling at me, something like, "But Zoe, you should just *do the box*. You have fans who will want it! Get it done!"

I know!

I *know!*

In the same way you know that I think you should just *do the thing* that you want to do, but you have reasons why you haven't yet.

It's more complicated when it's *our* thing, and the plan needs to be formed inside our own head. So much easier to map out a plan for someone else.

Which is why I bristle at things like positive affirmations or the power of positive thinking. I'm a super positive person, but I know that all of that can veer into *toxic* positivity pretty quickly.

But at the same time, I can look back in hindsight and recognize the power that setting an **aspirational mission statement** had as a business tool—what a difference that made for my career, after I took a Business Mastermind for Authors with Holly Darling.

This is where, as writers, we can dig into the value of words. Because if you say positive affirmations to me, I roll my eyes. If you say aspirational mission statement, I sit up a little straighter and lean in.

I've also heard this described as cognitive restructuring, and someone on Twitter called it a form of magic.

All of the above, including the "Let me hear you say you can!" barking instruction from gym teachers, are all roughly the same idea: **find a way to quiet the negative voices in your head and replace them with some deliberate, goal-oriented positive messaging.**

Easier said than done!

The mistake I make with this kind of positive thinking focus is not being specific enough. Also, it rarely works when someone else picks the mantra or mission statement. That gym teacher's opinion? Not one I've bought into.

Tackling anxiety and doubt is going to require a figured-it-out-myself kind of solution.

Sometimes just naming "what if" thoughts as anxiety and unfair doubt helps, too.

(I find this easier with anger. Anger = injustice. I see something as unfair, ergo, I am angry. Oh, hi anger. Something is wrong, and you see that. Naming it is sometimes enough that I don't need to feel like I have to take on all injustices myself.)

But like professional athletes, being a professional creative is largely a head game. And sorting that out is important to make space to do the work to get to your goals.

CHAPTER 20

DO THE WORK TO GET THERE

ONCE WE KNOW where we want to go, and we've mapped out a blueprint of bricks required to get there, all that is left to do is the actual work.

Which is, of course, the bulk of our job.

Doing it is huge.

Doing it is also hard.

Sticking with the plan may be easier if you have a visual reminder of why you have created the plan in the first place: your goals, posted on the wall of your workplace, or on the home screen of your phone or computer.

Remember your why.

And then prioritize writing above almost everything else.

WRITING PART-TIME

When I started writing fiction, I had a full-time job and two small children. Writing happened on my lunch breaks (two or three times a week) and every Saturday night. If I moved my work in progress (WIP) forward by 2000 words each week, I was thrilled.

One of the assumptions I make in this book is that you want to write multiple books a year. (If you don't, that's fine! Your goal profile should include an honest assessment of that, and make sure that your surround yourself with people who celebrate what you do want to write.)

So what does writing part-time look like in terms of producing multiple books a year?

It might mean writing novellas.

It might mean a little writing (almost) every day.

It might mean binge writing on the weekend, like I did.

It might mean learning to dictate in order to up your per hour word production.

SOME BOOK MATH TO CONSIDER:

1000 words a week, without fail, is 52,000 words a year (one category length novel, or two novellas)

2000 words a week, with two weeks of holiday, is 100,000 words a year (two category length novels, or four novellas, or eight novelettes)

3000 words a week, with four weeks off from writing, is 144,000 words a year (two full length novels, or six novellas, or twelve novelettes); at this pace, you could have a short story or novelette out every month

All of these are assuming a steady production pattern. Some people prefer to write, then take a break, then write again; and other people prefer to write seasonally, especially if their other career has a busy period. But I encourage you to figure out the book math that will match your goals, and adjust both accordingly until they match.

Also, production levels change over time! See my chart in chapter 11, Metrics Matter! I ramped up my production after my first two years of writing, and sustained that for a period of intense growth over three years, but it was not a long-term maintainable pattern.

WRITING FULL-TIME

I did an "ask me anything" post on Twitter a few weeks ago, and one question from Faye Delacour was about how I divide my time between writing and all the other work of being a published author.

Outside of the few weeks before a deadline, I have a max of about two or three hours of writing in me most days (and I don't write every day, but I do try to write frequently). So most of the time, I can do a 50-50 split between writing and all the other work. As I get closer to a deadline, writing ramps up, and everything else falls away.

And then around the release, it's the opposite. I don't get any writing done for a few weeks, because it's all marketing. But I think it balances out to about 50-50 over time.

As an aside: I don't count just being myself on social media as active brand management, though. If we include time spent making TikToks and Twitter threads, then the percentage shifts hard away from writing.

I think I write about fifteen hours a week at the best of times, and as I shared on my metrics table, in recent years, that has added up to 200,000-300,000 words per years.

Some people write more than that; some people write less. Being a "full-time writer" does not mean X number of words per year, because your career is built on your own priorities, pointed towards your own goals, and comparison will mostly just confuse our aim.

My big question is: if I want to write full-time, is *what* I am writing pointed in the direction of my long-term goals? If it's not, then it's time to re-work the plan.

. . .

ONCE WE HAVE a rough idea of what we can realistically produce, total word count wise, then the question is, where should we spend that effort?

In the master to-do list chapter, I shared a list of all the types of books and series to write.

All of these are equally valuable as product bricks in a plan; their relative value to *you* and *your goals* is what matters.

- Debut Book (ever, and also per pen name!)
- First Series
- Second Series
- Standalone Book
- New Genre Series
- Series 2.0
- Standalone Book that is a Project 2.0
- Series 3.0
- Collaborative Projects
- Serialized Works
- Novella series
- Cliffhanger (one big arc) series
- Trilogies inside a larger series

I introduced the concept of Series 2.0 in *Romance Your Brand*, and I've been getting questions about it ever since. A YouTube video I made where I confidently declared it as a career game changer didn't help! Well, it helped some people. But it created more questions than it answered, because I think it gave the impression that I believe Series 2.0 is better than any of these other bricks. It's not. Let's get into that in the next chapter.

CHAPTER 21

SERIES 2.0, AGAIN AGAIN

SERIES 2.0 IS a concept I came up with at some point, to differentiate for myself what Pine Harbour was to Wardham, as compared to SEALs Undone. I shared it in *Romance Your Brand*, almost word for word how I talked about it in an off-the-cuff Facebook post.

There wasn't a lot of depth to the analysis.

Then I elaborated a bit on it in *Romance Your Plan*, and *then* I made a YouTube video about it; what it was, but also, *what it was not.*

It also comes up literally every time I do a workshop, so obviously, people have questions.

So to start, let's recap what Series 2.0 is: an attempt to duplicate a previous series idea that resonated with readers, tightening the premise and refining the core story.

What is not (necessarily) is: a sequel, spin-off, genre shift, or shift in format or structure (ie, longer or shorter). All of those would be new series, which are important bricks in our wall. They may *lead* to a great Series 2.0 refinement idea!

Here is a drawing where I sketch out what I mean, in the framework model of a brick wall. At the bottom is our foundational mission statement or priority. On top of that we have our first layer of bricks: we've released some books, they're what the market expects, we're starting to see some reader delight.

On top of that we can stack (and remember, your layers will be your own choosing! This is just example): the start of an email list, a second series, a social media fan club, and more formats.

Then maybe we get a bit slicker with our marketing, and we focus more on building those reader capture mechanisms. All the while we're still writing, and the book brick on this layer happens to be a standalone book, maybe one that is geared to a holiday or super trope heavy. Good job, hypothetical writer!

So far this wall is well constructed and on the way, and it's only *now* that we try a Series 2.0.

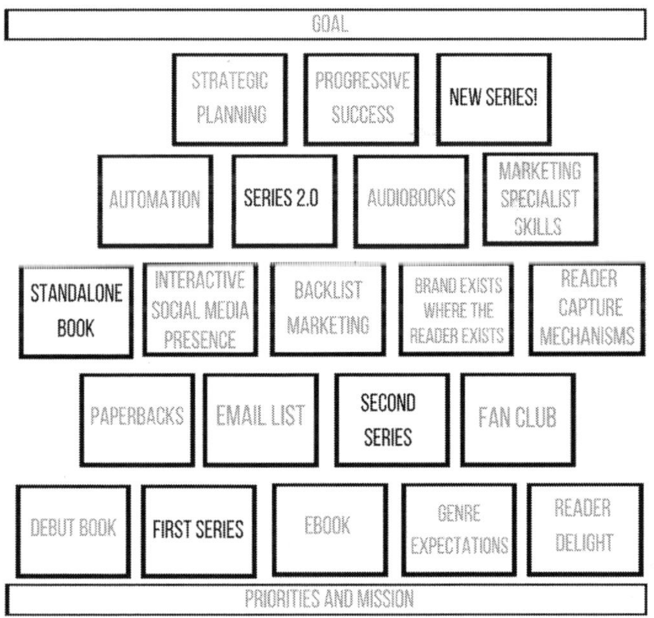

This Series 2.0 could be a re-boot on the core story of any of the books that came before it: your debut book, your first series, your second series, or that standalone. Whichever of those bricks has the best fandom (even a nascent one), and whichever creates the most exciting sizzle for you and readers: that's where you want to explore the Series 2.0 potential, because this will be a big attempt to deepen your brand in one specific spot.

Make sure you like that spot!

And then notice that in the last layer of bricks, I have sketched out writing a new series. Series 2.0 can be followed by any other type of project!

I hope that helps clarify that it's a tool in your toolbox, to pull out when you find a particularly good idea that reminds you of a previous project.

CHAPTER 22

THE PANDEMIC, YOUTUBE, AND HOW MUCH I LOVE TALKING TO PEOPLE

NAVIGATING A PLAN DURING THE WEIRDEST AND TOUGHEST OF TIMES

AT THE END OF 2019, I flew to Houston for Romance Author Mastermind. I spent four magical days at the Four Seasons hotel surrounded by my favourite kind of energy: no shame in having big goals, say your dreams with your whole chest, and build a plan to get there kind of energy.

We went out for fancy dinners. We networked. We listened, and laughed, and cried, and learned.

And then we went home, and got to work.

Two months later, in February 2020, I flew to Philadelphia for a writing retreat. Little did I know, it would be the last time I'd get on a plane (at least until the time of this book publishing in 2022). It certainly wasn't the last flight I had planned! Travel is high on my priority list, and I use it as reward and inspiration in equal measure.

I was going to Halifax to give a full-day, in-person Romance Your Brand workshop. I was going to Orlando for a book signing. And my family was going to Portugal, Spain, and Morocco for a much-anticipated summer holiday.

That was the plan. That was the carrot.

I had a long to-do list, and couldn't wait to spend the spring implementing it, earning those trips.

Then the news came out of China. Italy. New York. And on March 13, 2020, my kids came home from school with garbage bags filled with their belongings. Just in case.

That morning, I'd driven to the gym, my usual Friday routine, and met my personal trainer. They'd implemented some extra health precautions, and I told her if I didn't see her again for a while, I hoped we could pivot to online training.

I haven't been back to the gym since.

My usual Friday routine… I laugh now as I read that. I miss that routine so much. I don't think I could have handled those first six weeks if I'd known they would have actually lasted two years.

Especially because those first six weeks weren't bad at all for us. I'm deeply grateful that we were safe at home. I was interviewed by a Washington Post reporter about making bread with my kids. My husband built a work bench from scratch. We were healthy, and once we secured some toilet paper, our worries about supplies weren't that bad, either.

There would be harder periods—when my husband went back to work. When my kids went back to school. The endless wait for vaccines. As I write this, we're in the fifth wave here in Ontario, and it's the worst one yet. My kids have been exposed to COVID at school, and we're still waiting for my youngest to get his second dose of the vaccine. They're currently home from school, again.

It's a lot.

But my business hasn't been rocked the same way that it was in the winter of 2017/2018.

I have frameworks in place now to ensure that no matter what, I have options. I think about everything in terms of bricks. And if I can't write, then I find pebbles and stones to fill in that gap in the wall.

This book is a pebble. It won't sell nearly as many copies as a fiction novel (but sales aren't the only metric I track). For a while I made YouTube videos—starting a week after lockdown began in March 2020.

I felt the loss of that travel ahead of me, all those connections with readers and fellow writers *whoosh, gone.* So I recorded myself talking into my phone, and put it up on YouTube. I kept going for six months. Talking about lots of topics I've covered in these three non-fiction books, and things that came up along the way—like getting started on TikTok, and how to do email marketing.

I stopped making videos as abruptly as I started.

It served a purpose, filled a gap in my life, but it wasn't tied to my long term goals. I'm a writer, not a video content creator. (Some people are both; I am not.)

But I still missed talking to people. I found Clubhouse next, and started hosting an audio-only weekly live chat. This month I'll pass the one year mark of doing that. I may stop that abruptly at some point, too.

It's quite freeing to move on from bricks in the wall, to grab something new and try that instead. There are no rules about what your wall should look like.

SOMEHOW I HAVE WRITTEN three whole non-fiction books and not mentioned my favourite West Wing episode. This is very strange, because I mention it in almost every workshop I give.

"Give me the next ten words about how we're going to do it and I'll drop out of the race right now…". President Bartlet (The West Wing, season 4, episode 6 "Game On")

Lots of publishing advice falls into the ten word answer problem.

Backlist is king!

Write in series to retain readers!

Rapid release strategy is best!

Permafree is a game changer!

Whatever publishing path you take, whatever decisions you make, you'll have more success if you figure out the next ten words after those sound-bite bits of advice, and the ten after that, and align your decisions with what really matters to you, what you get excited about. Enthusiasm is more important than strategy.

Which brings us back to the pandemic, and sound-bite answers that are too simplistic to be accurate. One of them that I hear all the time is that "Twitter doesn't sell books."

I spent a lot of time on Twitter over the last two years. I can personally attest to the fact that it absolutely sells books, but the explanation how is slightly longer than ten words…

TWITTER SELLS BOOKS, AND OTHER CONTROVERSIAL OPINIONS

Or, why it's important to be clear about goals, processes, pathways, and other Super Sexy Publishing Things.

Social media sells books online, at online bookstores. This only works if your ebooks cost less than a burrito bowl.

Social media doesn't help you get a B&N end cap. It doesn't help you have a book named "book of the month" with a retailer. That's publishing team hustle.

Social media *can* help build librarian interest and support over time, but that's basically hand selling and relationship building. (The cocktail party analogy works well here)

You can probably achieve the same impact by networking in person with library heavy lifters at a con[1].

Five and ten word answers are killer, because they're too simplistic. "Social media doesn't sell books." Give us the next five words, and the five after that, and tell me what *does* sell books. That's more useful than declaring what doesn't work.

Another quote from the same West Wing episode, as spoken by C.J. Cregg, the press secretary: "Complexity isn't a vice." It's the reality in which we're all trying to do our thing.

Social media can sell books. Working diligently with a publisher can sell books. Both can flop so hard you need to get a job at Starbucks while you lick your wounds.

GOALS:

- #1 NYT bestseller?
- A Big Book every few years?
- Short and sexy novellas?
- Pulp fiction FUN?
- Work with a bucket list editor/publisher?
- Make writing a day job?

PROCESS:

- write books
- establish a platform
- write more books
- oh hey, is that the start of a peer network?
- getting closer! write another book
- layer. up. the. platforms!
- MAKE THE NEXT BOOK BETTER
- Almost there, do it again

PATHWAYS:

The way *you* sell books isn't the way *someone else is* going to sell books. There are so many ways to get there.

I can count on more fingers than I have the number of authors who have absolutely built Twitter into their primary platform, that when they post about their books here, they see real numbers move. Not dozens of books, but hundreds, and anyone who pretends that's not significant today is lying.

Hundreds of books moved in a day, from a tweet: that's power authors didn't use to have.

And not everyone likes the work that goes into building that platform. Not all of us (including me!) are suited to doing it. But it's a viable pathway. It just is.

It's also completely viable to use social media as your water cooler, nothing more, and build a bookselling career separate from that. This could be the traditional publishing path, or it could be indie publishing.

SOCIAL MEDIA PIMPING ≠ INDIE PUBLISHING

There are so many pathways to publishing success. I'm a process dork, so I tend to pay attention to more of them than most; I'm biased, 1000%, towards indie, because it's what has given me my career. It's not the only way. Not by a long shot. And it's not for everyone.

Some books don't have social media buzz and do well because they get internal buzz from the head buyer at Target or Walmart or B&N.

Some books don't have social media buzz but sell crazy well in ebook due to real reader word of mouth.

And some books sell a few copies a day, every single day, because of social media, and if you write enough of those, you can skip right past what other people think, and just keep doing your thing.

---

1. Cons are freaking expensive and social media just costs you time (and of course, a part of your soul)

CHAPTER 23

SPEAKING OF TWITTER...

I DIDN'T KNOW how to end this book, which is probably my way of saying I don't want to end this series (but I never want to end series). And I really do want to pivot back to only writing fiction for a while. So I took to Twitter and asked authors if they had any questions they wanted to contribute to the book, to be answered for everyone. Thank you to all who put their questions forward. These four threads directly relate to themes I've already addressed in the book, so I'm copying the questions and answers here in the hopes that they provide some additional context.

1. HOW DO I CHOOSE BETWEEN IDEAS? 2. WHEN IS IT BETTER TO START COMPLETELY FRESH AND NOT PICKUP A PARTIAL?

Anonymous

Zoe says:

1. Everything else being equal for *you* (equal enthusiasm), pick the project that feels most universally commercial; everything else being equal in terms of commercial viability, pick the

project that you have the most enthusiasm for (and/or excited terror about).

2. Almost always better to start fresh. Only go back to a partial when it will not leave you alone.

IT TAKES ME WILDLY DIFFERENT AMOUNTS OF TIME TO COMPLETE BOOKS, AND THIS MAKES IT HARD FOR ME TO PREDICT A SCHEDULE. I'M TORN BETWEEN WORKING ON COMPLETING BOOKS ON A SET TIMELINE OR NOT TYING GOALS TO DATES. WHAT ARE SOME WAYS TO APPROACH THIS?

Charlotte P.

Zoe says:

One option: draft or even fully complete books before you add them to a publishing schedule; So the publishing schedule happens on a completely different timeline from the writing.

Another: build the mystery into your brand (if publishing path allows it).

Things option 2 sparks for me: marketing that is more focused on books post-release rather than building up to a launch; marketing the author brand vs the individual titles; creating reader community space that celebrates the unknown and anticipation

WHAT ARE SOME EASY WAYS TO BUMP YOUR PROFITS TO THE NEXT LEVEL? OR WHERE DO YOU SPENT MONEY TO GET THE MOST BANG FOR MY BUCK AND REACH YOUR FINANCIAL GOALS? (NEWSLETTERS, ADVERTISING, COVERS, FIRST IN SERIES FREE, ETC.)

@jennyredford

Zoe says:

Writing a series 2.0, or a standalone single title release

(project 2.0), that resonates with your existing fans is the strongest income game changer.

Once you do that, keep doing it. Everything else builds on that lever, and makes the profit greater. But without that, it's hard.

There are a lot of things I can recommend that will work after you have a strong series 2.0 that will not work beforehand.

DO YOU HAVE ANY THOUGHTS ON HOW NOVELS VS NOVELLAS IMPACTS YOUR GOALS, IN TERMS OF TIME SPENT WRITING, SALES, LONG-TERM READER ENGAGEMENT, ETC.?

@bymiamarshall

Zoe says:

This depends on sub-genre, but in broad strokes, novellas are fast acting levers to push for momentum and velocity, and novels are longer burning brand building products.

Everyone has different strengths when it comes to writing, but for me, it is also easier/faster to write 3x30k novellas than 1x90k novel, and I can sell each of those for more than 1/3 the 90k novel... so there is some short term $ to be made in novellas that is very appealing.

But five years on, looking back, novels earn more over the years, are steadier, and there are better promotional tools for them (specifically BookBub).

So if you feel some kind of tension between the two, that's probably accurate, and if possible, I'd suggest writing both. NOT in the same series, but in separate series.

(The same universe is fine, but interstitial novellas between novels sell WAY worse than a separate series of steady length novellas will.)

And the final question thread comes in three parts:

I OFTEN HEAR PEOPLE SAY I SHOULD HAVE A FIVE YEAR PLAN BUT HOW DOES THAT WORK WHEN EVERY DECISION I MAKE ABOUT THE NEXT BOOK IS BASED ON THE PREVIOUS WORK? WHAT A WRITE IN TWO YEARS DEPENDS ON WHAT PERFORMS BEST THIS YEAR.

@RancherNikki

Zoe says:

I prefer to have a five year plan where every day is the first day in that plan. (So it's a five year projection that is being adjusted frequently)

SO IS THERE ANYTHING THAT STAYS CONSISTENT IN THAT PLAN? OR ARE YOU MAKING BROAD LONG-TERM PLANS (EX. WRITE MORE ON-BRAND BOOKS) AND ONLY GET MORE DETAILED SHORT-TERM (EX. WRITE BOOK X NEXT)?

@megan_linden

Lots can stay consistent! Let me try to workshop this in a Twitter appropriate length... right now, today, if I ask myself the Q, "5 years from now, what do I want to have written?" The answer is Canadian-set romance. Small town as Zoe, high-heat hockey as Ainsley.

The small town answer is not new; that remains consistent with previous plans. The hockey romance is a pivot from what I thought last year that I might be writing as Ainsley. So that's not the same as past plans.

From there, I check in on the plan, and figure out how to morph. I need to finish Bull of the Woods (the final Frisky Beavers book), readers are expecting that. All right; can I change it to point back to hockey more than I intended originally?

On the Zoe side, this check-in reminds me to play whack-amole with non-small town ideas that pop up. Throw a Scooby snack at them, distract them and hope they wander away.

And then tomorrow is the first day in that "new" plan, which is a continuation of the old plan, but with some modifications based on a new long-term vision.

Maybe I release that hockey series, and it's fine, but I realize, oops, it's not actually what I want to write. (I don't think that'll be the case, but maybe? Gotta stay loose.)

Then I ask the Q again, take a new bearing, and realign the plan.

I LOVE THE FIRST Q, BECAUSE THE "WANT" PART MAY CHANGE DOWN THE LINE, BUT IT'S NEVER UNTRUE IN THE MOMENT, WHICH MAKES IT ALMOST IMPOSSIBLE TO FAIL. THE PLAN IS, ULTIMATELY, CONNECTED BOTH TO THE PRESENT & THE FUTURE AT THE SAME TIME, WHICH MAKES IT FLEXIBLE. I LOVE THAT!

@megan_linden

Right! And pivoting over and over again isn't a problem ... it's narrowing in, over time, on a straighter path.

CHAPTER 24
CONCLUSION

THIS BOOK of lists is going to end with another list. After spending a lot of the book talking about myself, now I want to talk about you about your plan to romance your goals.

- Take stock of what you have already achieved **(it is likely more than you know)**
- Be honest about what you want to accomplish
- Make that your goal right now
- Plan a step-by-step, brick-by-brick approach to get there
- It doesn't matter how big or small your bricks are
- You can always start over, but the framework will be the same
- **Pick the path you have the most enthusiasm for**

You can do this.

All the best,
Zoe York
your peer on this journey

ALSO BY ZOE YORK

What Once Was Perfect (Wardham)

Love in a Small Town (Pine Harbour)

Fall Out (SEALs Undone)

A Viking's Peace (Vikings in Space)

Ruined by the SEAL (Hot Caribbean Nights)

Skinny Dipping Dare (SEALs at Camp Firefly Falls)

Reckless at Heart (Kincaids of Pine Harbour)

written as Ainsley Booth

Hate F*@k (Forbidden Bodyguards)

Prime Minister (Frisky Beavers)

written as Gigi Ford (first released as Ainsley Booth)

Love Your Dreams (Girls Who Love Girls)

For a complete list of my books after this book is published, please visit my websites:

www.zoeyork.com

www.ainsleybooth.com

www.gigiford.com

APPENDIX: DIAGRAMS

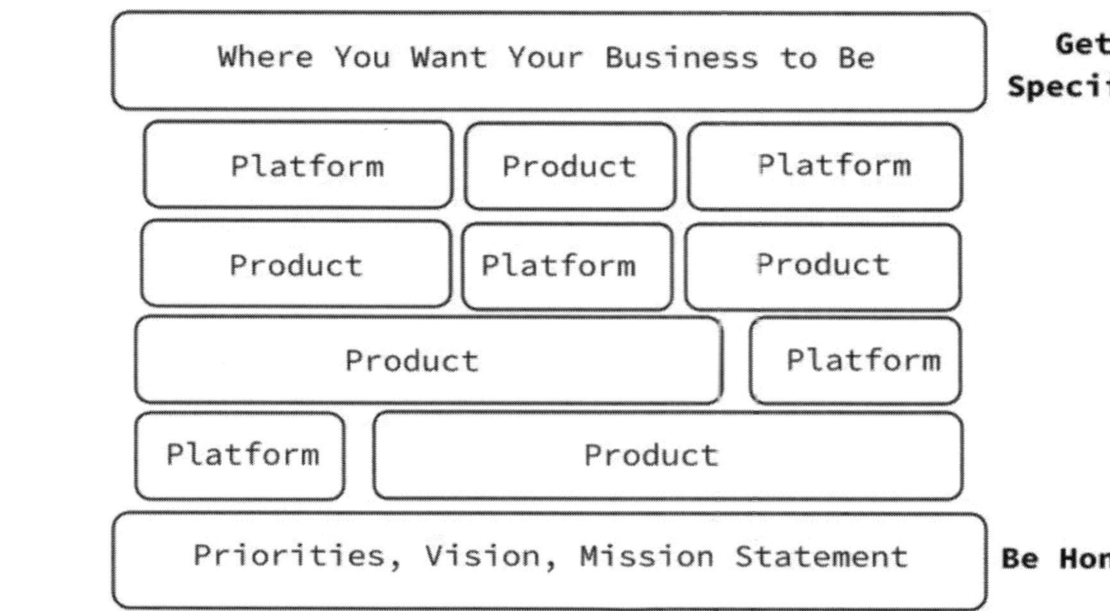
The Framework
Where You Want Your Business to Be
Get Specific
Platform
Product
Platform
Product
Platform
Product
Product
Platform
Platform
Product
Priorities, Vision, Mission Statement
Be Honest

building a series, building a career: my plan from 2013-2015

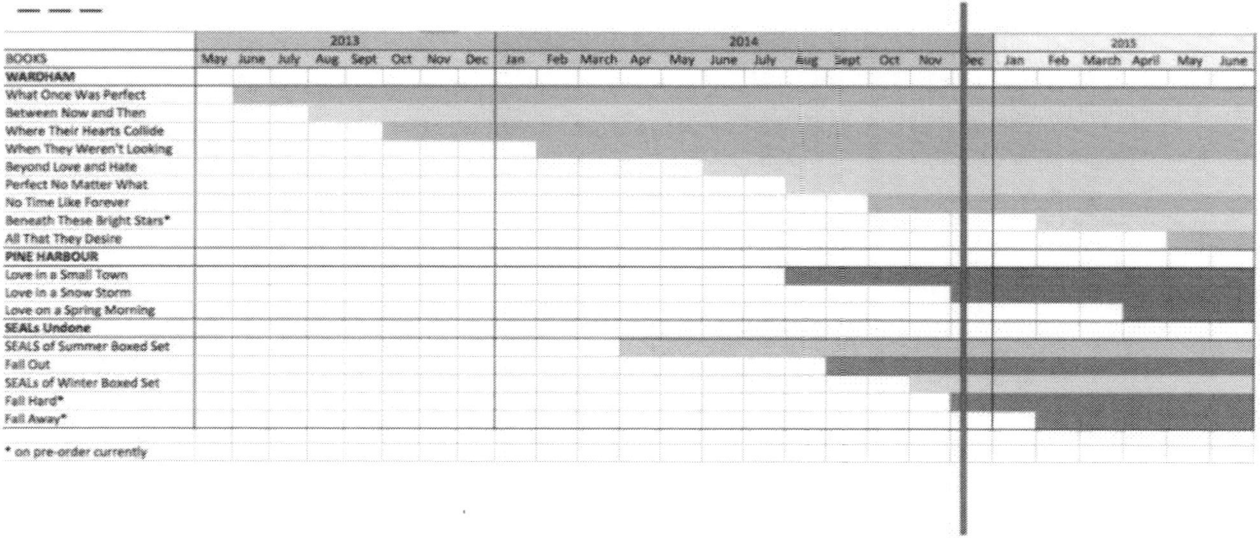

	2013								2014												2015					
BOOKS	May	June	July	Aug	Sept	Oct	Nov	Dec	Jan	Feb	March	Apr	May	June	July	Aug	Sept	Oct	Nov	Dec	Jan	Feb	March	April	May	June
WARDHAM																										
What Once Was Perfect																										
Between Now and Then																										
Where Their Hearts Collide																										
When They Weren't Looking																										
Beyond Love and Hate																										
Perfect No Matter What																										
No Time Like Forever																										
Beneath These Bright Stars*																										
All That They Desire																										
PINE HARBOUR																										
Love in a Small Town																										
Love in a Snow Storm																										
Love on a Spring Morning																										
SEALs Undone																										
SEALS of Summer Boxed Set																										
Fall Out																										
SEALs of Winter Boxed Set																										
Fall Hard*																										
Fall Away*																										

* on pre-order currently

	2013	2014	2015	2016	2017	2018	2019	2020	2021
WORDS PUBLISHED (ANNUAL)	122,000	391,000	498,000	466,000	511,000	211,000	213,000	215,000	328,655
NEW BOOKS PUBLISHED	3	8	13	13	11	6	4	5	7
SERIES WITH FREE BOOKS AVAILABLE	1 (NOVELLA)	1	3	4	5	6	8	8	8
BONUS WORDS WRITTEN						5000	5000	5000	25,000
ZOE NEWSLETTER	652	1854	6798	11,002	14,882	21,733	32,618	39,781	44,381
AINSLEY NEWSLETTER			2236	4286	8074	9929	9516	9152	12,532
SECRET ALTER EGO NEWSLETTER									1500

Made in the USA
Middletown, DE
16 May 2022